Gifts from the Kitchen

Gifts
from the Kitchen

By Norma Myers
and Joan Scobey

Illustrated by Jean La Vigna

DOUBLEDAY & COMPANY, INC.
GARDEN CITY, NEW YORK

ISBN: 0-385-02477-0
Library of Congress Catalog Card Number 72–96250
Copyright © 1973 by Norma Myers and Joan Scobey

To good food
and good friends
and the occasions
that bring them together

Acknowledgments

Too MANY COOKS may spoil the broth, but they make light work for recipe collectors. For sharing favorite recipes with us we thank Ellen Buzbee, Beverly Cunningham, Shirley Fields, Arlene Fine, Marilyn Fishel, Ellin London, Cecile K. Marek, Muguette Martel, Joan Philips, Rosie Scheffreen, and Joan Vasiliades.

We are indebted to Susan Myers for helping test the contents of this book, and to our three other taster-critics, Wendy, Sarah, and Rick.

Most particularly, we thank Tina Petermann and Babette Schmidt, owners of Éclat Housewares, 6 Spencer Place, Scarsdale, N.Y. 10583, Patricia Agre, and Carol Davis.

Finally, we wish to note the contribution of Harriet Langsam, who played the Muse, of Mary Whitesides, who designs and creates recycled metal containers for Consumer Action Now, Inc., 30 East 68 St., New York, N.Y. 10021, and of Jane Wilson, for her patience and support.

Contents

Gifts from the Kitchen xi

1 Gift Containers 1
2 Nice and Easy 7
3 The Hors d'Oeuvres Tray 37
4 The Soup Kettle 61
5 The Bread Basket 75
6 Dinner in a Dish 97
7 The Relish Tray 127
8 The Sauceboat 153
9 The Cookie Crock 181
10 The Cake Plate 205
11 The Candy Jar 231
12 Holiday Giving 251

Appendix A Mailing Food 281
Appendix B Sources 285
Index 287
Recipes for items in initial caps may be located by consulting the Index

Gifts from the Kitchen

A GIFT FROM THE KITCHEN is twice blessed; it gives pleasure to the giver as well as to the receiver. Whether you are an experienced cook or an enthusiastic novice, there is great satisfaction in reviving a treasured family recipe or trying a new treat to share with an old friend or new neighbor.

The custom of presenting food to both friend and stranger has ancient roots. Although the actual food itself has varied in different societies, gifts of bread and salt are traditional the world over. Whatever the particular offering, the gift itself indicated acceptance of a stranger and affection for a friend.

In keeping with the tradition of presenting gifts of food, we are adding a new dimension by making the containers themselves an integral part of the gift. Chosen with care and imagination, containers may be bottles, crocks, and baskets, or miniature chests, sea shells, and pencil holders. They may be as simple as a tray or as unexpected as a watering can, as modest as a bandanna or as special as a Spode cup. In every case they offer an extra bonus to be kept and enjoyed long after your gift of food is gone. That bonus may be an imported measuring cup which will remain in the kitchen, a pail which will later find its way to the beach, or a vase to hold flowers.

Opportunities for gourmet gifts are many. Some are traditional, others are entirely personal. Consider a present for a dinner or weekend hostess; a sick friend in need of supper for the family; Christmas, Easter, and other holidays; family birthdays and special occasions; children's gifts for teachers; the church supper and the PTA fair. Anyone intrigued by this kind of gift giving might happily celebrate Columbus Day by presenting a beautiful crock of pesto Genovese, or might ignore the calendar altogether and make a *tourtière* for a homesick Québecois. Your youngster can make a "Nice and Easy" recipe to take on a visit to grandmother while you put together a "Dinner in a Dish" for a neighbor down with flu.

The kinds of food that lend themselves to such presentations are almost as numerous as the occasions. They must meet few requirements: they must be portable and they must have the necessary keeping quality. In the past, a kind neighbor often brought a ham or turkey next door to make moving day and its aftermath more tolerable. But today, since we are more knowledgeable about food, and we enjoy regional and ethnic dishes from all over the world, gifts from the kitchen can reflect our new sophistication.

This book, then, brings together a group of recipes that travel well and are in themselves of interest. Because so much of the fun of giving gifts from the kitchen lies in the creative touch of the cook, we have avoided prepackaged ingredients whenever possible. On the other hand, while retaining the integrity of classic recipes, we have tried to simplify procedures. And we have chosen dishes suitable for both expert and beginner cooks.

After selecting the recipe you want to follow, adapt the quantities to your own needs. We often like to make small amounts of some delicacies and then package a pair of them together. Or we may double the quantity of a particular family favorite and enjoy the extra portion at home.

At the end of some recipes you will find "A Note" with our recommendations for cooking, serving, or storing. You need use it only as a guide for writing your own note, for a dish you have made with care deserves to have your personal stamp from mixing bowl to label.

The same is true of the gift container. While the range of packaging ideas in the book is wide, be encouraged to present your gifts with a style and charm all your own, using the suggestions at the beginning of each chapter, as well as the information in "Gift Containers."

Naturally, we hope that you and your friends enjoy these particular gifts from the kitchen, but even more, we hope you will adopt the joyous concept of making some special, treasured, or original recipe, coupling it with an imaginative container, and presenting a gift from the kitchen uniquely your own.

NORMA MYERS
JOAN SCOBEY

Gifts from the Kitchen

1

Gift Containers

ONCE YOU HAVE ADOPTED the joyful habit of presenting both foods and their containers, you'll notice all sorts of objects that can bear your gifts from the kitchen. Walk through a department store and your mind's eye will put cookies in a soup tureen, praliné in a ginger jar, spiced nuts in an antique tea caddy. You'll want to fill a hanging flower pot with muffins, a wicker garden tote with summer's preserves, and a pewter tankard with cheese sticks.

Enjoy the fun of collecting containers as you go to a

country auction or garage sale, rummage in a thrift shop or flea market, pass a gift shop window, browse through mail order catalogues (see Appendix B). The fun of "containerizing" is to recognize a cocktail shaker as the perfect way for carrying soup and a window planter for toting bread or loaf cakes. The art is putting aside odd plates and bowls that catch your fancy, baskets, boards, boxes, and trays of all sizes, shapes, and materials. Collect gay napkins, dish towels, and aprons to wrap around loaves and muffins. Lay in a store of whisks, mixing spoons, pastry brushes, and other utensils to tie on. The trick of collecting containers is to pick up a pair of ramekins, a trio of covered soup dishes for gift giving when you cannot find a whole set for your own use. And if chipped and broken pieces have depleted a set of your china, don't bemoan the loss but rescue the few good pieces for gift giving.

You'll find containers in florist shops, housewares departments, kitchenware boutiques, gift shops, in card shops and toy stores, in basket bazaars, where paper and party accessories are sold, at auctions and county fairs. Look for desk and bar accessories, tools and implements for the garden and home, cooking and serving pieces. Above all, keep an open and imaginative mind for the unexpected object that can hold, wrap, or adorn your gift from the kitchen.

Here are some suggestions.

Cookware and kitchen accessories

egg cup and coddler	bean pot
mortar and pestle	soufflé dishes, large and small
chemical retort	sea shell

Cookware and kitchen accessories

sugar scoop
wok
recipe box
colander
hollow rolling pin
kitchen towel
baking sheet
covered omelet pan
measuring cup
Mason jar

mesh salad basket
molds for pâté, fish, brioche, etc.
canister set
apothecary jar
quiche pan
cutting board
pastry bag
muffin tin

Serving pieces

sugar shaker
bouillon and soup cups
pitchers of all sizes
thermos bottle
cream and sugar
bun warmer
crock
tray
bread board
teapot
straw basket
relish tray
wine cooler
parfait glass
punch bowl
cruet
trivet
ginger jar
honey pot

pots de crème
jam pot
salad bowls in variety
crystal jug
mugs and tumblers
ramekin
plate
cheese board
carafe
set of stacking dishes
server dome
picnic hamper
brandy snifter
bar glasses
punch cups
tureen
tea caddy
mustard jar
wine basket

Accessories

lacquer and brass boxes

miniature chest

terrarium

pencil holder

pewter tankard

ice bucket

tissue holder

Toby jug

cigarette box

shaving mug

fish bowl

ash tray

mustache cup

cocktail shaker

cachepot

decanter

From the florist

flower pot

watering can

window box

bird feeder

hanging flower pot holder

garden tote basket

planters of all kinds

From the toy store

tambourine

fireman's hat

football helmet

wheelbarrow

stacking blocks

book or school bag

doll's cradle

Christmas stocking

lunch pail

tom-tom or drum

cowboy's hat

sand pail

toy wagon

dump truck

doctor's bag

open train car

doll's suitcase

Miscellaneous

apron

flask

fishing gear box

hat box

bandanna

tool box

paint pail

paper totes and other paper
goods

Creative packaging

Charming and inexpensive containers can also be created by recycling cans, jars, decanters, and bottles. You can dress them up with bright colored plastic tape, pine cones, leaves, ribbons, decals, and decoupage. You can wrap them in colored cellophane, wallpaper and fabric samples, ticking and other material, or gaily patterned self-adhesive plastic. Or you can leave them unadorned save for an attractive label.

Environmentalists who are handy with tools can make scoops and mugs from metal soup cans. To make the scoop, remove the top of the can with a can opener, cut the scoop shape out with a metal shears, and drill a hole in the center of the bottom so a wooden handle can be screwed to the scoop. To make the mug, remove the bottom of a soup can with a can opener, cut a handle from another soup can, and solder both ends of the handle to the sides of the can.

Using more imagination than cash, you can creatively package a kitchen product in a checked napkin, brightly printed dish towel or apron, a burlap bag, or even a bright colored paper tote or string bag. Add your personal touch by tying on a whisk, slotted wooden spoon, cookie cutter, or other utensil.

Packaging tips

· Don't forget to label the contents of all containers, and add "A Note" whenever necessary, with information on cooking, storing, shelf life, reheating, freezing, and just generally enjoying the food.

· Use fabric tape to seal the lids of covered soup bowls,

sugar servers, jam pots, and other objects whose lids may not fit tightly.

•Cover and seal open-topped containers with plastic wrap.

•Keep a supply of plastic bags in all sizes on hand. You will need them to store cakes, cheese balls, some meat dishes, and other items that are best kept air tight. They are also useful for protecting the interior of containers.

•Buy pretty cardboard and metal boxes in different sizes at notions counters and variety stores. Stock up during holiday seasons when variety is greatest.

•Make liberal use of newsprint for wrapping, using the comics for children's gifts and financial and editorial pages for their parents.

•Wrap jars, balls, cylindrical and irregular shaped objects in a pouf package. Place the object in the center of a napkin or piece of gift wrap or colored cellophane large enough to accommodate it. Bring the four ends together and tie with yarn or ribbon at the top of the object.

•Wrap candy individually in plastic wrap for best keeping qualities.

•Keep cookies in airtight containers for maximum freshness. When mailing cookies, wrap individually in plastic wrap.

2

Nice and Easy

THIS POTPOURRI of fun and easy treats is custom designed for anyone short of time or culinary experience who wants to prepare a gift from the kitchen. Simple out of proportion to the results, these recipes are quick enough for busy career girls and impatient youngsters, yet sufficiently sophisticated to please a gourmet who enjoys the beauty of a *beurre composé* on his poached turbot.

They also lend themselves to a wide variety of unexpected containers. To get you started, here are some packaging suggestions.

Heap nuts, croutons, dried fruit confections in a pair of antique egg cups, a Lucite recipe box, oriental lacquer box, or a milk glass mustard jar.

Store flavored sugars and herb salts in a bright enamel sugar shaker, a diminutive bean pot, or a pair of covered bouillon cups.

Pack flavored butters in a small ginger jar, a trio of tiny soufflé dishes, or an old shaving mug.

Tote liquids in an antique flask, stoppered glass pitcher, or decorative thermos.

Mound confections in a lovely sea shell, a ceramic pâté mold, or a large sugar scoop, and secure with colored cellophane.

Fill a silver-lidded egg coddler or imported jam pot with pesto or duxelles.

Present cashew or peanut butter in a marvelous antique mustache cup.

PESTO GENOVESE
For 1 pound of spaghetti

The name of this glorious sauce for spaghetti comes from the phrase *al pesto,* which means "by pounding," since a mortar and pestle was the original way to prepare this Italian specialty from Genoa. Be sure to make pesto in the spring and summer when you can grow basil in your own garden or, at least, find it readily available in the market.

2 cups loosely packed fresh basil leaves, chopped
2 tablespoons olive oil
2 tablespoons butter, melted
1 clove garlic
¼ cup pine nuts (pignoli)
1 teaspoon salt

1. Put all the ingredients into a blender and, using a spatula to scrape the sides of the container, process until the mixture is a thick purée.
2. Refrigerate the pesto, covered, with a thin film of olive oil.

A NOTE Heat the pesto gently and cook the spaghetti *al dente.* Drain the spaghetti well and toss it with the pesto; serve with ½ cup freshly grated Parmesan cheese. You can also add a dollop of pesto to minestrone or spread it on tomato halves and broil. Pesto keeps well in the refrigerator for a week or in the freezer for several months. Before storing in a tightly capped container, cover surface of pesto with a thin film of olive oil.

DUXELLES
Makes 1 cup

This is a seasoned mushroom filling and a delightful way to flavor sauces, stuffing, omelets, and many an elegant fish or meat dish.

½ pound mushrooms, finely chopped
2 tablespoons butter
2 tablespoons oil
3 tablespoons finely chopped green onions or shallots
Pinch freshly grated nutmeg
Salt
Pepper

1. Place the chopped mushrooms in a dish towel or large handkerchief, then twist and squeeze to extract as much moisture as possible from the mushrooms.
2. Heat butter and oil, then sauté the mushrooms and minced onions or shallots over medium high heat, stirring frequently. Within 10 minutes the liquid should be absorbed and the mushrooms light brown. Add nutmeg, salt, and pepper to taste.
3. Refrigerate in a covered container.

A NOTE   Duxelles adds a fresh seasoned mushroom flavor to stuffings and sauces, is a superb filling for a savory omelet or beef Wellington. Keep it covered in the refrigerator for a week or freeze it.

FLAVORED CROUTONS

A PACKAGE OF FLAVORED CROUTONS helps any hostess turn a familiar soup or salad into something special. A selection of the following would be a happy addition to any pantry shelf.

PARMESAN CROUTONS
Makes 1½ cups

6 slices firm white bread, crusts removed
4 tablespoons salted butter
½ cup freshly grated Parmesan cheese
1 teaspoon paprika

1. Cut bread into ½-inch squares.
2. In a large heavy frying pan, melt the butter and sauté the bread cubes over medium high heat until lightly browned on all sides.
3. While still warm, toss the buttered bread cubes with the cheese and paprika in a paper or plastic bag.
4. Drain on paper towels and let cool.

A NOTE Parmesan croutons are splendid in onion and spinach soups, scalloped tomatoes, and all manner of casseroles. Keeps well in an airtight container in a cool place for several weeks.

GARLIC CROUTONS
Makes 1½ cups

6 slices firm white bread, crusts removed
2 tablespoons olive oil
2 tablespoons butter
2 large cloves garlic, split

1. Cut bread into ½-inch squares.
2. In a large heavy frying pan, heat oil and butter with the garlic and, when hot, remove the garlic cloves.
3. Sauté the bread cubes over medium high heat until lightly browned on all sides.
4. Drain on paper towels and let cool.

A NOTE Crunchy and flavorful garlic croutons are a classic component of Caesar salad, and add just the right touch to gazpacho. Crush them to stuff tomatoes Provençale and to garnish baked eggplant. Keeps well in an airtight container in a cool place for several weeks.

HERBED CROUTONS
Makes 1½ cups

6 slices firm white bread, crusts removed
4 tablespoons salted butter
1 teaspoon dried parsley
1 teaspoon dried tarragon
1 teaspoon dried rosemary

1. Cut bread into ½-inch squares.

2. In a large heavy frying pan, melt the butter over medium high heat. Crush the herbs finely between your hands or in a mortar and pestle and stir them into the hot butter.

3. Sauté the bread cubes in the butter until lightly browned on all sides.

4. Drain on paper towels and let cool.

A NOTE   Herbed croutons add not only a subtle taste but a marvelous contrasting texture to creamed soups such as lobster, shrimp, and tomato bisque, *potage* St. Germain, vegetable soups, and fish chowders. If you like asparagus, broccoli, or cauliflower topped with bread crumbs, crush the croutons in a bag with a rolling pin, sauté in a little butter, and you will have improvised a sauce Polonaise.

HERBED SALTS

FLAVORED SALTS are the happy marriage of complementary seasonings, each enhancing the others. Their touch is subtle, their light green color superb.

BASIL SALT
Fills a standard 3-ounce spice jar

½ cup table salt, non-iodized
¾ cup finely cut fresh basil leaves

1. Blend ingredients vigorously with mortar and pestle for 3 minutes to release the herb essence.
2. Spread on a small cookie sheet or foil to dry.

A NOTE   Basil salt enlivens cooked or fresh tomatoes, cold salads, seafood, and eggs.

DILL SALT
Fills a standard 3-ounce spice jar

½ cup table salt, non-iodized
¾ cup finely chopped fresh dill sprigs

1. Blend ingredients vigorously with mortar and pestle for 3 minutes.
2. Spread on foil or a cookie sheet to dry.

A NOTE   Try this on shrimp, cucumbers, potato dishes, and string beans.

SALT AUX FINES HERBES
Fills a standard 3-ounce spice jar

½ cup table salt, non-iodized
4 tablespoons finely chopped fresh parsley leaves
4 tablespoons finely chopped fresh tarragon leaves
4 tablespoons finely chopped fresh chives

1. With mortar and pestle, mash all ingredients vigorously for about 3 minutes until the salt turns light green and the herbs are well blended.
2. Spread on foil or a cookie sheet to dry.

A NOTE   A delightful seasoning on poultry, eggs, soup, fish, salads, and vegetables.

SEASONED SALT
Makes ⅔ cup

6 tablespoons table salt, non-iodized
1 tablespoon sugar
1 tablespoon paprika
1 teaspoon pepper
1 teaspoon onion powder
½ teaspoon garlic powder
1 teaspoon dry mustard
1 teaspoon allspice
1 teaspoon coriander

Mix all ingredients together until well blended.

A NOTE   This is a tangy salt to try on beef, hard-boiled eggs, veal, and salads.

CITRUS SUGARS

CITRUS SUGARS are simple to prepare, beautiful to look at, and perform culinary magic when added to beverages, desserts, fruit dishes, and baked desserts.

LEMON SUGAR
Makes 1 cup

2 tablespoons grated lemon zest (outer rind)
1 cup superfine sugar

Combine the ingredients and store in a tightly covered jar.

A NOTE   A lively flavoring for tea, iced or hot, of course, and for your favorite fruits, fresh or cooked.

ORANGE SUGAR
Makes 1 cup

2 tablespoons grated orange zest (outer rind)
1 cup superfine sugar

Combine the ingredients and store in a tightly covered jar.

A NOTE   Sweeten grapefruit, hot cereals, French toast, and cold drinks with this.

CASHEW BUTTER
Makes ⅔ cup

Cashew butter is a sublime treat for everyone who loves nut spreads and is addicted to cashews.

4 tablespoons vegetable oil
1 cup salted cashew nuts

1. Pour 1 tablespoon of the oil in the bottom of the blender and add half the nuts. Blend at high speed. Then add the remaining oil and nuts, following the same procedure. Use a spatula to keep the ingredients flowing into the cutting blades.
2. Blend until you reach the desired consistency or "crunchiness."

A NOTE This nut butter has no preservatives and is not homogenized, so store in the refrigerator and stir, if necessary, before serving.

PEANUT BUTTER
Makes ⅔ cup

Homemade peanut butter bears the same relation to its store-bought counterpart as home-baked bread does to most packaged bread. Commercial peanut butter is rarely made with the germ of the nut, which is so rich in minerals, vitamins, and proteins, just as most breads are made without the germ of the grain. Health-conscious friends and peanut butter afficionados of all ages will enjoy this.

1 cup salted peanuts
2 tablespoons vegetable oil

1. Add nuts slowly to blender container, alternating with the oil, and process at high speed. Use a spatula to keep ingredients flowing into the cutting blades.
2. Blend until the desired consistency or "crunchiness" is reached.

A NOTE Since there are no preservatives in this peanut butter, store it in the refrigerator and stir before serving, if necessary, because it is not homogenized.

COLD FLAVORED BUTTERS
(*BEURRES COMPOSÉS*)

THESE SAVORY BUTTERS are marvelous gifts. They are easy to make and add a delightful fillip to grilled meats and fishes. Experienced cooks will also use them to enrich a sauce or soup, or to baste meat, fish, or poultry. A busy hostess may not have time to make these butters for herself, but will surely delight in having them at hand.

Whenever possible, use fresh herbs, for they give an incomparable flavor. If they are not available, generally 1 teaspoon of dried herb is the equivalent of 1 tablespoon fresh. The secret of making these butters lies in creaming the butter thoroughly with wooden spoon, wire whisk, or electric mixer before adding the other ingredients, and then continuing to cream until the mixture is well blended.

ANCHOVY BUTTER
Makes ½ cup

½ cup sweet butter
1 teaspoon lemon juice
2 teaspoons anchovy paste
Pinch cayenne pepper

1. Cream the butter thoroughly.
2. Beat in the lemon juice drop by drop, and then the anchovy paste and pepper, creaming until mixture is well blended.

A NOTE This butter adds a salty tang to baked and broiled fishes, so gauge the salt you use in your recipe accordingly. Keep covered in the refrigerator.

BERCY BUTTER
Makes ⅔ cup

1 tablespoon finely chopped shallots
½ cup dry white wine
½ cup sweet butter
1 tablespoon finely chopped fresh parsley or 1 teaspoon
    dried parsley flakes
Salt
Pepper

1. In a small heavy saucepan, cook the shallots in the wine over medium high heat until reduced to half the volume, then set aside to cool.
2. Cream the butter thoroughly and add the parsley, mixing until well blended.
3. Add the cooled wine mixture and season to taste with salt and pepper.

A NOTE Top broiled steaks or chops with a dollop of Bercy butter just before you bring them to the table. The butter freezes well, but if kept in the refrigerator more than 3 or 4 days the flavor of the parsley will fade.

GARLIC BUTTER
Makes ½ cup

4 large garlic cloves
½ cup water
½ cup sweet butter

1. Peel garlic cloves and boil them in the water for 2 minutes. Drain, dry on a paper towel, then crush in garlic press or mortar and pestle.
2. Cream the butter thoroughly, then add the crushed garlic and mix together until well blended.

A NOTE Try this garlic butter in preparing fish and sea-food, as well as in a crusty loaf of bread.

HONEY BUTTER
Makes 1 cup

½ cup sweet butter, softened
½ cup honey
2 tablespoons heavy cream

Cream softened butter thoroughly, then add honey and cream, beating well with a wooden spoon or in an electric mixer.

A NOTE This is perfection atop French toast, waffles, pancakes, hot puddings, and gingerbreads.

LEMON HERB BUTTER
Makes ½ cup

½ cup sweet butter
1 teaspoon lemon juice
2 teaspoons grated lemon rind
1 teaspoon finely minced fresh parsley leaves or
   ½ teaspoon dried parsley flakes
1 teaspoon minced chives
⅛ teaspoon dried tarragon

1. Cream the butter thoroughly, then add the lemon juice drop by drop, beating continuously.
2. Stir in the lemon rind, parsley, chives, and tarragon until well blended.

A NOTE This is marvelous served on steaming asparagus or any broiled or poached fish as it arrives piping hot at table. To keep this herbed butter at the height of its flavor, freeze it if it isn't used within 3 or 4 days.

MAÎTRE D'HÔTEL BUTTER
Makes ½ cup

½ cup sweet butter
1 teaspoon lemon juice
½ teaspoon Worcestershire sauce
2 teaspoons finely chopped parsley or 1 teaspoon dried
   parsley flakes
Salt
Pepper

1. Cream the butter thoroughly, then add the lemon juice drop by drop, the Worcestershire sauce, and the parsley, creaming until all the ingredients are well blended.

2. Season to taste with salt and pepper.

A NOTE   A professional finishing touch to broiled chops or a sizzling steak.

MARCHAND DE VIN BUTTER
Makes ⅔ cup

1 tablespoon chopped shallots
½ cup red table wine
1 teaspoon meat extract
½ teaspoon lemon juice
1 tablespoon finely chopped parsley leaves or 1 teaspoon
dried parsley flakes
¼ teaspoon coarsely ground black pepper
Pinch dried tarragon
½ cup sweet butter

1. Cook shallots in red wine quickly over medium high heat until the volume is reduced to half. Remove from heat.

2. Add meat extract, lemon juice, parsley, pepper, and tarragon, stirring to blend. Let cool.

3. Cream butter thoroughly, then add wine mixture slowly, continuing to beat until light and fluffy.

A NOTE   Use this classic butter on beef, both broiled and roasted. Like other herb butters, it freezes well and should not be refrigerated more than a week if you want to enjoy the full flavor of the herbs.

MUSTARD BUTTER
Makes ½ cup

½ cup sweet butter
2 teaspoons Dijon mustard

Cream the butter thoroughly and slowly add the mustard, continuing to beat until well blended.

A NOTE   This is excellent spread on thin slices of rye or pumpernickel bread for many kinds of open-faced sandwiches or hors d'oeuvres, or add a dollop to broiled fish or grilled meat.

ORANGE BUTTER
Makes ⅔ cup

½ cup sweet butter
1 small clove garlic, mashed
Grated rind 1 small lemon
Grated rind 1 orange
2 tablespoons frozen orange juice concentrate
Salt
Pepper

1. Cream butter thoroughly and add mashed garlic, rind of lemon and orange, the orange juice concentrate, beating until well blended.

2. Season to taste with salt and pepper.

A NOTE   What a flavor this adds when used in preparing baked or broiled chicken and roast duck!

ROQUEFORT BUTTER
Makes ¾ cup

½ cup sweet butter
1 drop Tabasco sauce
¼ teaspoon Worcestershire sauce
¼ cup crumbled Roquefort or blue cheese

1. Cream butter thoroughly and slowly add Tabasco and Worcestershire sauces, beating until well blended.

2. Add crumbled cheese and blend until smooth.

A NOTE   Spoon this onto piping hot grilled hamburgers or atop a meat loaf on its way to table; broil on rounds of French bread; or spread on thin slices of rye bread for an hors d'oeuvres.

HERBED VINEGARS

HERBED VINEGARS are easy to prepare and improve with age. A variety is especially nice for pantry shelves.

TARRAGON VINEGAR
Makes 2 pints

1 cup fresh tarragon sprigs
3¾ cups white wine vinegar
2 large tarragon sprigs

1. Place tarragon sprigs in a clean quart jar and press down with wooden spoon to crush herb slightly.
2. In a stainless steel or enamel saucepan, bring vinegar just to boiling point. Pour at once over tarragon leaves. Cap tightly and let steep 2 weeks.
3. Strain contents of jar into two sterilized pint bottles into each of which a large sprig of tarragon has been placed. Cork tightly and store at room temperature.

A NOTE   Use to make salad dressing.

BASIL VINEGAR
Makes 2 pints

1 cup fresh basil leaves
3¾ cups red wine vinegar
2 fresh basil sprigs

1. Place basil leaves in a clean quart jar and press down with a wooden spoon to crush herb slightly.

2. In an enamel or stainless steel saucepan, bring vinegar just to the boiling point. Pour at once over the basil leaves. Cap tightly and let steep 2 weeks.

3. Strain contents of jar into two sterilized pint bottles into each of which a large fresh sprig of basil has been placed. Cork tightly and store at room temperature.

A NOTE   Use for marinating tomatoes, string beans, and other vegetables.

MIXED HERB VINEGAR
Makes 2 pints

½ cup fresh rosemary leaves
½ cup fresh thyme leaves
4 shallots, peeled and sliced
1 large sprig parsley
12 peppercorns
3¾ cups cider vinegar

1. Place rosemary, thyme, shallots, parsley, and peppercorns in a clean quart jar and press them down with a wooden spoon to crush herbs slightly.

2. In a stainless steel or enamel saucepan, bring the vinegar just to the boiling point. Pour at once into the jar of crushed herbs. Cap tightly and let steep 2 weeks.

3. Pour the vinegar through a fine strainer into two sterilized pint bottles into each of which a fresh sprig of rosemary or thyme has been placed. Cork tightly and store at room temperature.

A NOTE   Mixed herb vinegar makes a zingy salad dressing, and is especially nice in a vinaigrette sauce.

GARLIC VINEGAR
Makes 2 pints

10 large cloves garlic, crushed
1 teaspoon salt
3¾ cups cider vinegar

1. Place crushed garlic and salt in a clean quart jar.
2. In a stainless steel or enamel saucepan, bring vinegar just to the boiling point. Pour at once over garlic. Cap jar tightly and let marinate 10 days.
3. Strain contents of jar into two sterilized pint bottles. Cork tightly and store at room temperature.

A NOTE   This vinegar is a particularly nice component of dressing for Caesar salad.

PRALIN
Makes 1 cup

Pralin, also called praline powder, is a candied nut garnish for sophisticates.

1 cup superfine sugar
½ teaspoon vanilla
1 cup blanched almonds

1. In heavy skillet, melt sugar and vanilla over low heat, stirring constantly.
2. When syrup is light brown, add the almonds, stirring until nuts are well coated.
3. Pour onto buttered cookie sheet and let stand until cool and brittle.
4. Then chop or crush with a rolling pin.

A NOTE   Sprinkle over ice cream, custards, mousses, or fruit desserts. And it's a spectacular garnish around the sides of any frosted layer cake. Store pralin in a covered container in a cool dry place.

TOASTED COCONUT
Makes 1 cup

1 can (4 ounces) flaked coconut

1. Preheat oven to 300 degrees F. and line a cookie sheet with foil.
2. Spread coconut evenly on foil sheet and bake, stir-

ring occasionally, until flakes are uniformly light brown, about 20 to 30 minutes.

3. Cool and store in a tightly capped container.

A NOTE   Toasted coconut is an elegant accessory for many different foods. Sprinkle it over fruit cup, serve it as a condiment with curry dishes, and for a smashing dessert, serve vanilla ice cream with your favorite liqueur crowned with toasted coconut bits.

CONFECTIONS

FRUIT AND NUT CONFECTIONS, favored by many hostesses for their holiday tables, are welcomed happily all year long.

NUTTED PRUNES
Makes 24

24 pitted prunes
½ cup superfine sugar
1 tablespoon grated lemon zest (outer rind)
¼ cup chopped walnuts

1. Steam prunes in the top of a double boiler for 5 minutes until they are tender and plump. Set aside to cool.
2. Combine sugar, rind, and nuts for stuffing.
3. Make an indentation in the prunes and fill with the stuffing.

A NOTE A tightly covered container will keep these fresh for weeks.

GINGER DATES
Makes 24

1 tablespoon chopped candied orange peel
1 tablespoon chopped crystallized ginger
¼ cup superfine sugar
¼ cup chopped almonds
1 tablespoon Madeira wine
24 pitted dates

1. To prepare stuffing, combine orange peel, ginger, sugar, nuts, and moisten with Madeira.
2. Slit dates lengthwise and fill.

A NOTE Store in an airtight container for long life and good eating.

ORANGE SUGARED NUTS
Makes 1 cup

½ cup walnut halves
1 cup pecan halves
½ cup sugar
¼ cup water
1 teaspoon grated orange rind

1. Put all ingredients in a large heavy skillet and cook over medium heat until water evaporates and nuts have a sugary look.
2. Pour nuts onto a greased baking sheet, separating them quickly with a fork. Cool and store in a covered container in refrigerator.

A NOTE If you can keep these out of the hands of nibblers, store in a covered container in the refrigerator or in the freezer. They will keep several weeks in an airtight container.

SALTED NUTS
Makes 2 cups

1 tablespoon butter
1 tablespoon oil
2 cups assorted nuts
1 teaspoon seasoned salt

1. Preheat oven to 300 degrees F.
2. Melt the butter and mix with the oil.
3. In a bowl, toss the nuts with the butter and oil until well coated.
4. Spread the nuts out on a cookie sheet and bake for 15 minutes, or until lightly browned, stirring occasionally. Remove to paper towels and drain.
5. Sprinkle nuts with salt and toss. Store them in a tightly capped container.

A NOTE Store in a tightly covered container in the refrigerator or freezer. Keeps well for several weeks.

SPICED WALNUTS
Makes 1½ cups

1 egg white
1 tablespoon water
½ cup sugar
½ teaspoon allspice
½ teaspoon cinnamon
½ teaspoon salt
½ pound walnuts

1. Beat egg white and water until foamy but not stiff.

2. In a large bowl, mix the sugar, allspice, cinnamon, and salt together.

3. Put the nuts in the egg white and stir to coat thoroughly. Remove them with a slotted spoon and toss well in the sugar mixture.

4. Bake on a greased cookie sheet in a preheated 300 degree F. oven for 1 hour, stirring the nuts every 15 minutes.

A NOTE Great with drinks, of course, but an unexpected delight when crushed and sprinkled over ice cream or fresh fruit compote. Store in a tightly covered container in the refrigerator for several weeks.

SANGRIA
Makes 1 quart

This fruited and refreshing drink from Spain, traditionally made with red wine and native fruit, is a splendid summer gift.

2 fresh peaches, sliced
2 oranges, sliced
2 tablespoons sugar
1 quart Spanish burgundy or California Mountain Red

In the bottom of a tall pitcher, press fruit and sugar together with a long wooden spoon, then add wine.

A NOTE   Serve chilled or over ice, and if you like a sparkling wine, add a split of club soda at the last minute.

3

The Hors d'Oeuvres Tray

ONE OF THE NICE THINGS about hors d'oeuvres and appetizers is that they often double as luncheon dishes. A cheese log or ball, coupled with a bowl of fresh fruit, provides an appetizing lunch or a Continental dessert. A salmon quiche is served with salad for lunch or in thin wedges with drinks before dinner. This versatility will surely please any hostess.

Packaging the array of dishes presented in this chapter

offers beguiling opportunities, for there is an almost end-
less variety of possible containers. For instance:

Heap meatballs and cold vegetable dishes into a fluted
mold, or into a bright red imported plastic bowl accompanied by salad tongs.

Pack shrimp pesto or crab meat remoulade into a crystal jug, a fish mold, or even a small fish bowl.

Stuff marinated olives in tankards or tumblers, a
unique mustache cup, or in recycled and decorated
orange juice cans or peanut butter jars.

Seal cheese balls in plastic wrap and nestle in a wine
basket, hanging flower pot holder, or bun warmer. Stow
the plastic-wrapped cheese log in a tool box or garden
tote.

Pack pâté in a Lucite flower pot, a Toby jug, brioche
mold, or any size and shape of crock.

Present the quiches on a pretty antique plate, any tray
of tole, straw, or bright-colored plastic, or on a round
domed cheese board. For a child, lay the pizza quiche in
a tambourine and protect it with plastic wrap or cellophane.

PÂTÉ À LA NORMANDE
Makes 3 cups

This pâté combines the special flavors of Normandy, the province of apple orchards and dairy farms.

1 onion, chopped
¼ pound butter
1 small apple, peeled and chopped
1½ pounds chicken livers, cut in pieces
¼ cup applejack or Calvados
2 hard-boiled eggs, cut in pieces
Heavy cream
Salt
Pepper

1. Sauté the onion in 3 tablespoons of the butter until golden. Add the chopped apple and cook until soft. Process the mixture in the blender and set aside.
2. Add the remaining butter to a frying pan and sauté the chicken livers until brown on the outside and pink in the center.
3. Warm the apple brandy and flame the chicken livers. Add this to the mixture in the blender jar and process with the eggs, blending until the mixture is smooth. Add cream as needed to keep the blades moving. Process in two batches if necessary.
4. Season to taste with salt and pepper.
5. Pack pâté in small crocks or a well-oiled 3-cup mold and refrigerate.

A NOTE Pâté won't keep longer than 2 or 3 days in the refrigerator, so if you want to freeze this, seal the top of the pâté with a thin film of clarified butter.

CHICKEN LIVER PÂTÉ
Makes 4 cups

This is a favorite recipe of many a Jewish grandmother who traditionally served it to her Friday evening dinner guests.

2 pounds chicken livers
Chicken stock to cover
4 hard-boiled eggs
1 large onion, finely chopped
6 tablespoons butter or chicken fat
Salt
Pepper

   1. Poach chicken livers in lightly simmering stock for 10 minutes, then drain.
   2. In a food mill, process livers with eggs.
   3. Sauté onion in butter or chicken fat and blend into the liver mixture.
   4. Season to taste with salt and pepper.
   5. Pack pâté in small crocks and refrigerate.

A NOTE   Serve within 2 days or freeze, covering the top of the pâté with a thin film of clarified butter to seal.

COUNTRY PÂTÉ
Serves 6 to 8

When a French family goes on a *pique-nique,* more than likely the hamper contains an elegant pâté. This one combines pork and veal, laced with cognac.

2 tablespoons butter
1 large clove garlic, mashed
1 onion, finely chopped
1 pound ground pork
1 pound ground veal
½ cup ground pork fat
2 eggs, lightly beaten
1 teaspoon dried thyme
1 teaspoon dried marjoram
¼ teaspoon allspice
¼ cup cognac
Salt
Pepper
1 pound salt pork, thinly sliced

1. Preheat oven to 350 degrees F.
2. Melt the butter in a large frying pan and sauté the garlic and onion until golden. Transfer to a large mixing bowl.
3. To the mixing bowl, add the pork, veal, pork fat, eggs, thyme, marjoram, allspice, and cognac, and mix thoroughly.
4. Season to taste with salt and pepper. To test for sea-

soning, sauté 1 tablespoon of the meat mixture in a frying pan and taste; because of the pork content, do not taste uncooked pâté.

5. Line a 1-quart baking dish with slices of salt pork and fill it with meat mixture. Cover the top with additional slices of salt pork. Place a heavy cover on the baking dish, set it in a shallow pan of water, and bake for 1½ hours.

6. Cool pâté to room temperature, keeping the weighted top on the pâté.

7. Unmold on a serving plate and remove the surrounding pork slices. Garnish with parsley, pimiento strips, and black olives.

A NOTE   Slice thin for an excellent first course or luncheon dish and serve with crusty French bread. Serve within 1 week or freeze.

CURRIED SHRIMP SPREAD
Makes 1½ cups

Curry and potted shrimp are two British favorites, here combined.

1 cup chopped cooked shrimp
2 tablespoons chopped scallions (white part only)
½ cup heavy cream
6 tablespoons butter, softened
½ teaspoon dry mustard
1 teaspoon curry powder
1 tablespoon lemon juice
Salt

1. Process the shrimp, scallions, and cream in the blender until smooth, adding more cream if necessary to keep the blender blades from clogging.

2. In a mixing bowl, cream the butter, mustard, and curry powder well together.

3. Slowly beat in the puréed shrimp mixture. Add lemon juice and salt to taste.

4. Pack the spread in small crocks and refrigerate until firm and well chilled. Garnish with a whole shrimp.

A NOTE Serve with simple crackers or melba toast. This spread keeps a week in the refrigerator but the curry powder loses its potency when frozen.

SMOKED SALMON SPREAD
Makes 2 cups

A great favorite at cocktail time, this spread extends that expensive delicacy, smoked salmon, to serve a large gathering.

8 ounces cream cheese, softened
1 cup sour cream
½ pound smoked salmon, sliced and cut in thin strips
2 tablespoons finely chopped scallions
2 tablespoons finely chopped fresh dill sprigs or 1 table-
    spoon dried dill weed
1 tablespoon lemon juice

1. Combine cream cheese and sour cream thoroughly, then stir in remaining ingredients.
2. Pack in a covered crock.

A NOTE   Garnish with a sprinkling of chopped fresh dill, and serve with thinly sliced black bread and sliced cucumbers. Keeps for several days in refrigerator.

ANCHOVY SPREAD
Makes 1½ cups

Inexpensive and delicious, easy to prepare, a delight with crudités—what more could an hors d'oeuvres be?

¾ pound cream cheese, softened
¼ pound sweet butter, softened
½ small onion, grated
2 cans flat anchovies, drained
1 teaspoon paprika

1. Combine all the ingredients and mix thoroughly.
2. Pack in a covered crock.

A NOTE   Use as a stuffing for celery stalks. Keeps 1 to 2 weeks in the refrigerator.

LIPTAUER KÄSE
Makes 1½ cups

This cheese spread is a delectable contribution from Middle Europe. It was originally made with liptauer, a goat's milk pot cheese from which it got its name, and is here adapted to American taste.

4 ounces pot cheese or small curd dry cottage cheese
4 ounces cream cheese, softened
4 ounces sweet butter, softened
1 tablespoon grated onion
½ teaspoon crushed caraway seeds
1 teaspoon anchovy paste
1 teaspoon Dijon mustard
1 teaspoon paprika
2 tablespoons flat beer

1. Combine all the ingredients and blend thoroughly.
2. Pack in two covered crocks and refrigerate.

A NOTE   Serve with thinly sliced black bread. This keeps well in the refrigerator for a week.

CHEESE BLENDS

UNLIKE MANY CHEESES which must be used at their flavor peak, nut-wrapped cheese blends make delightful gifts because they may be prepared ahead and mellow with age.

CAMEMBERT LOG
Serves 6

7 ounces Camembert
4 tablespoons butter, softened
1 tablespoon cognac
½ cup almonds, toasted and finely chopped

1. Remove rind from cheese while cold, then set aside to soften.
2. In a small bowl, cream the cheese and butter well, then blend in the cognac.
3. Refrigerate mixture until firm enough to form into a log.
4. Roll the cheese log in the chopped nuts until well coated.

A NOTE   This versatile log is equally good with cocktails or for dessert served with fruit and crackers.

DANISH CHEESE BALL
Serves 8 to 10

½ pound Danish blue cheese, softened
¼ pound butter, softened
3 ounces cream cheese, softened
1 teaspoon grated onion
1 tablespoon cognac
¾ cup toasted and chopped pecans

1. Cream together the blue cheese, butter, cream cheese, grated onion, and cognac.
2. Refrigerate mixture until firm enough to form into one large ball.
3. Roll the cheese ball in the chopped nuts until completely covered.

A NOTE   Sealed tightly in plastic wrap, this freezes beautifully for future entertaining.

CHEDDAR CHEESE ROUNDS
Makes 60 rounds

The idea of brown-and-serve baked goods is here adapted to hors d'oeuvres. Who wouldn't be pleased to have this refrigerator roll of tangy rich cheese wafers on hand?

4 tablespoons butter
4 ounces sharp Cheddar cheese
1 teaspoon Dijon mustard
½ teaspoon onion powder
1 teaspoon salt
Dash cayenne pepper
½ cup flour, sifted
½ cup caraway seeds

1. Melt butter.
2. Grate the cheese into a large mixing bowl. Add the melted butter, mustard, onion powder, salt, and pepper, and mix until thoroughly blended.
3. Add the flour and mix well.
4. Form into a log 1½ inches in diameter, and roll it in the caraway seeds.
5. Package in cellophane or plastic wrap and refrigerate or freeze.

A NOTE   Slice the log thinly and bake the cheese rounds an inch apart on a greased baking sheet at 375 degrees F. for 10 minutes, or until golden. The cheese log freezes well and keeps for weeks in the refrigerator, so use as needed.

CRAB MEAT REMOULADE
Makes 2 cups

An elegant first course, especially charming when served individually in shells.

12 ounces frozen crab meat
1 cup Remoulade Sauce

    1. Defrost crab meat and drain well.
    2. Combine crab meat and remoulade sauce in a bowl and chill overnight in refrigerator.

A NOTE   Keeps well in the refrigerator for several days. Garnish the serving bowl with cherry tomatoes and parsley.

SHRIMP IN PESTO SAUCE
Serves 4 to 6

This dill pesto, an unusual and delightful variation of the more traditional pesto made with basil, is fittingly served with seafood.

½ cup olive oil
½ cup clam juice or liquid used in cooking the shrimp
2 large cloves garlic
1 cup fresh dill sprigs
½ cup fresh parsley leaves
Salt
Pepper
2 pounds cooked shrimp

1. Process the olive oil, clam juice, garlic, dill, and parsley in a blender until thoroughly combined.

2. Add salt and pepper to taste.

3. Combine the sauce with the shrimp and chill thoroughly.

A NOTE   Serve shrimp in individual sea shells and garnish with a sprinkling of pignoli nuts for an added touch of Italy. Keep refrigerated and serve within 2 days.

MARINATED COCKTAIL OLIVES
Makes 2 cups

These are marvelous to have on hand, especially since they mellow and improve with age.

1 jar (4¾ ounces) pitted green olives
1 can (5¾ ounces) pitted black olives
3 large cloves garlic, split
¾ cup Mixed Herb Vinegar
Pepper
1 sprig fresh basil or 1 tablespoon dried basil
¾ cup olive oil

1. Drain olives.

2. Combine all ingredients in a bowl. Cover and refrigerate at least 3 days.

A NOTE   Superb for cocktails, of course; also an admirable garnish for summer salads. Remove garlic cloves before serving. Keep refrigerated.

MARINATED MUSHROOMS
Serves 6 to 8

These occupy an honored spot on the antipasto tray, along with spiced meats, fish, and hard-boiled eggs.

⅔ cup olive oil
3 tablespoons Mixed Herb Vinegar
3 tablespoons lemon juice
¼ cup chopped scallions
1 small clove garlic, finely chopped
Salt
Pepper
1 pound large mushrooms, cleaned and sliced

1. In a large mixing bowl, combine oil, vinegar, lemon juice, scallions, garlic, salt, and pepper.
2. Toss the mushroom slices gently in this dressing until well coated. Refrigerate several hours or overnight.

A NOTE   Chill well before serving on a bed of watercress. Keeps in refrigerator for several days.

COLD MIXED VEGETABLES

VARIOUS COMBINATIONS of vegetables and diverse seasonings characterize the following cold mixed vegetable recipes. All are felicitous accompaniments to simply prepared meat dishes, serve as elegant luncheon fare, and, of course, for hors d'oeuvres. They also keep well several days under refrigeration.

VEGETABLES VINAIGRETTE
Serves 8

3 cups chicken stock
½ cup oil
½ cup white wine
1 tablespoon salt
12 peppercorns
1 onion, in quarters
2 cloves garlic, split
1 bay leaf
3 cups broccoli florets
3 cups cauliflower florets
3 cups diagonally thinly sliced carrots
¼ cup Mixed Herb Vinegar

1. In a large saucepan, simmer chicken stock, oil, wine, salt, peppercorns, onion, garlic, and bay leaf for 20 minutes. Strain the marinade and return to pot.

2. Bring the strained marinade to a boil and add the broccoli. Cook uncovered 3 to 5 minutes, or just until crisp tender. Remove broccoli with a slotted spoon to a colander and rinse in cold water. Place in a large bowl.

3. Add the cauliflower to the boiling marinade and cook uncovered for 3 to 5 minutes, or just until crisp ten-

der. Remove cauliflower with slotted spoon to colander, rinse in cold water, and add to broccoli in bowl.

4. Add carrots to boiling marinade and cook uncovered 5 minutes, or just until crisp tender. Remove carrots with slotted spoon to colander, rinse in cold water, and add to bowl with other vegetables.

5. Reduce the marinade to 1 cup by boiling briskly. Let cool, then add herb vinegar. Pour the dressing over mixed vegetables and refrigerate.

A NOTE This colorful and tasty appetizer also doubles as a splendid salad with luncheon cold cuts. Garnish with chopped fresh parsley and chives. Keeps in refrigerator for several days.

SALADE MÉDITERRANÉE
Makes about 6 cups or serves 8

⅔ cup oil
2 large cloves garlic, split
½ cup finely chopped onions
½ pound small mushroom caps
1 medium eggplant, peeled and coarsely chopped
1 tablespoon dried basil
1 can (17 ounces) imported Italian-style tomatoes
1 package (9 ounces) frozen artichoke hearts, thawed
1 teaspoon salt
Pepper
⅓ cup lemon juice
½ cup pitted black olives

1. In a large heavy saucepan, heat oil and add garlic, cooking over medium heat until cloves are golden. Remove garlic.

2. Add onions, mushrooms, and eggplant, and cook until onions are transparent.

3. Stir in basil, then add tomatoes, artichokes, salt, and pepper. Cook over medium heat for 5 minutes. Cool.

4. Add lemon juice and black olives and toss.

A NOTE Equally good served warm or cold, and as an accompaniment to grilled meats. Keeps in refrigerator for several days.

RATATOUILLE
Serves 6 to 8

1 eggplant (about 1½ pounds)
Salt
6 tablespoons olive oil
1 small zucchini, sliced
2 cups sliced onions
1 green pepper, sliced
1 red pepper, sliced
2 large cloves garlic, mashed
1 large can (35 ounces) Italian-style tomatoes, drained
    or 6 medium tomatoes, peeled, seeded, and quartered
1 teaspoon sugar
4 tablespoons chopped fresh parsley
4 tablespoons chopped fresh basil leaves or 1 tablespoon
    dried basil
Pepper

1. Peel and coarsely chop the eggplant and place in mixing bowl. Sprinkle with salt and let stand half an hour at room temperature. Wipe dry with paper towels.

2. In a large frying pan, heat the oil and sauté the eggplant, zucchini, onions, peppers, and garlic until the onions are golden. Transfer the mixture to a 4-quart ovenproof casserole.

3. Add to the frying pan the tomatoes, sugar, herbs, salt, and pepper, and cook over medium heat uncovered for about 20 minutes.

4. Preheat oven to 350 degrees F. while the tomatoes are cooking.

5. Add the tomato mixture to the casserole and combine all ingredients. Bake about 40 minutes, or until the vegetables are tender and most of the liquid is absorbed.

A NOTE A delicious dish of Provençal origin, excellent served hot or cold. Keeps in refrigerator for 1 week or in freezer for several months.

QUICHES

HERE ARE TWO UNUSUAL VARIATIONS of the traditional French custard pie. The salmon quiche is delicately herbed, the pizza quiche quite spicy, but both are particularly suitable as hors d'oeuvres.

SALMON QUICHE
Makes one 9-inch pie

2 eggs
½ cup Mock Hollandaise Sauce
1 tablespoon minced fresh dill sprigs or 1 teaspoon dried dill weed
2 teaspoons dried minced onion reconstituted in 1 tablespoon water
Salt
Pepper
1 can (7½ ounces) salmon, drained and flaked
1 pie shell (9 inch), baked

1. Preheat oven to 375 degrees F.
2. In a mixing bowl, beat the eggs lightly and add the mock hollandaise sauce, dill, onions, salt, pepper, and salmon. Mix well.
3. Pour the mixture into a prepared piecrust and bake for 25 minutes.

A NOTE   Warm the quiche in a 325 degree F. oven for 20 minutes and serve in thin wedges as an hors d'oeuvres. This is also a splendid luncheon dish served with a tossed green salad and a French bread.

PIZZA QUICHE
Makes one 9-inch pie

½ pound sweet Italian sausages
4 tablespoons salad oil
1 medium onion, chopped
2 cloves garlic, chopped
1 cup well drained Italian-style canned tomatoes
¼ cup finely chopped fresh parsley
1 teaspoon oregano
1 teaspoon dried basil
Salt
Pepper
2 eggs
2 egg yolks
4 tablespoons heavy cream
1 pie shell (9 inch), baked
4 ounces mozzarella cheese, shredded

1. Preheat oven to 350 degrees F.
2. In a small saucepan, cook the sausages in simmering water for 15 minutes. Remove them and pierce the skins in several places to drain excess fat.
3. Brown the drained sausages in 2 tablespoons of the oil. Drain them on paper towels and cool. Cut into ¼-inch slices, and set aside.
4. In the remaining 2 tablespoons of oil, sauté the chopped onion and garlic until golden.
5. Add the tomatoes, parsley, oregano, basil, and salt

and pepper to taste, and cook uncovered until most of the liquid is absorbed and the mixture is thickened.

6. In a large bowl, beat together the eggs, egg yolks, and cream. Add the tomato mixture to it and combine well.

7. Place the sausage slices evenly on the bottom of the baked pie shell. Pour in the tomato mixture and sprinkle the cheese on top. Bake for 30 minutes.

A NOTE   Heat for 20 minutes in a 325 degree F. oven and serve in thin wedges.

SWEET AND SOUR MEATBALLS
Makes thirty-six 1-inch balls

Invariably, cocktail meatballs are the chafing dish favorite, and this pungent sweet and sour version is particularly popular.

1 egg
¼ cup flavored bread crumbs
2 tablespoons water
1 tablespoon finely chopped fresh parsley
Salt
Pepper
1 teaspoon Dijon mustard
1 pound ground beef
1 small clove garlic, finely chopped
1 small onion, finely chopped
2 tablespoons butter
3 tablespoons oil
4 tablespoons brown sugar
4 tablespoons lemon juice
2 tablespoons soy sauce
2 tablespoons ketchup
1 tablespoon cornstarch
1 teaspoon ginger
1 cup beef bouillon

1. In a large bowl, beat the egg lightly with a fork, then add bread crumbs, water, parsley, salt, pepper, mustard, and beef. Mix well.
2. Sauté garlic and onion in butter until golden. Stir into meat mixture.

3. Form meat into bite-size balls about 1 inch in diameter.

4. In a large heavy skillet, heat oil and brown the meatballs on all sides. Remove meatballs when browned and drain all but 1 tablespoon of the oil in the pan.

5. In the skillet, combine the brown sugar, lemon juice, soy sauce, ketchup, cornstarch, and ginger, stirring until they are well mixed. Then add the beef bouillon and cook, stirring, until thickened.

6. Add the meatballs to the sauce and simmer for 10 minutes.

A NOTE   Warm the meatballs over medium heat in a chafing dish. Keeps in refrigerator for several days or in freezer for several months.

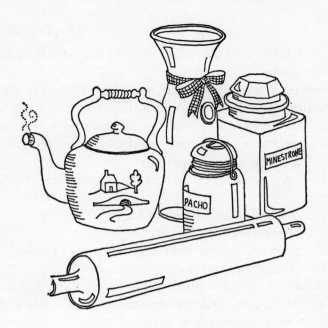

4

The Soup Kettle

"SOUP OF THE EVENING, beautiful soup!" sang the Mock
Turtle in *Alice in Wonderland,* ruefully acknowledging
the pleasures of the soup kettle.

Soups of all kinds make delightful gifts. Chilled or
steaming, for summer or winter, soup in any form is a
liquid asset. Some provide just the right start to an elegant dinner, others the substance of a hearty meal. Here,
then, is a group that should meet every gift occasion,

from a hearty winter dinner soup to a luscious summer fruit consommé.

Obviously, soup containers must meet certain conditions: they must be leakproof, liquidproof, and spillproof. While this necessarily limits usable containers, an imaginative packager will find possibilities in unexpected places. Here are some suggestions:

Fill a stoppered cocktail shaker, carafe, or chemical retort.

Use a teapot, corking its spout for the trip.

Pour into one section of a canister set.

Fill a glass rolling pin with soup before it's pressed into service with ice water at the pastry counter.

Consider a set of stacked glass candy jars, using the bottom for the soup and the top section for accompanying croutons. Seal with masking tape.

Recycle and decorate coffee cans, jars, holiday decanters.

Pack in Mason jars for the friend who enjoys canning.

And, of course, always available are apothecary jars of all shapes and sizes, corked and stoppered.

FRESH MUSHROOM SOUP
Serves 8

Here is a delicate, lightly creamed consommé to enhance the flavor of fresh mushrooms, an elegant start to a meal.

6 tablespoons butter
4 scallions, finely chopped
3 tablespoons flour
6 cups chicken stock
1 pound mushrooms, stems chopped and caps thinly
    sliced
1 tablespoon lemon juice
Salt
Pepper
1 cup heavy cream
2 tablespoons dry sherry
Freshly grated nutmeg

1. In a heavy 3-quart saucepan, melt 3 tablespoons of the butter and sauté the chopped scallions until soft.

2. Stir in the flour to form a smooth paste and continue stirring over moderate heat 2 minutes. Gradually add the chicken stock and blend thoroughly.

3. Add the mushroom stems (reserve the caps) and continue cooking for 30 minutes.

4. Meanwhile, in a large frying pan, melt the remaining 3 tablespoons of butter and sauté the sliced mushroom caps. Sprinkle with the lemon juice and add salt and pepper to taste.

5. When the stock has finished cooking, process in blender until smooth. Return to saucepan and add the mushroom caps and their juices. Let simmer 5 minutes.

6. Add the cream, sherry, and a few gratings of fresh nutmeg.

A NOTE   To serve, heat well but do not boil. Garnish with a dollop of whipped cream and toasted slivered almonds. Keeps in refrigerator for several days.

SPINACH SOUP
Serves 6

For those who especially like spinach, this light soup is heavenly, and an unusual change from more customary cream of spinach concoctions.

4 tablespoons butter
1 medium onion, finely chopped
1 small clove garlic, finely chopped
1 pound spinach, well washed
4 cups chicken stock
2 tablespoons chopped fresh parsley
1 teaspoon dried marjoram
Salt
Pepper

1. Melt butter and sauté onions and garlic until golden. Remove mixture to blender jar and set aside.
2. Cook spinach in a small amount of water 5 minutes. Drain and add cooked spinach to blender jar.
3. Process contents of blender jar until puréed. Transfer mixture to large saucepan.
4. Add the chicken stock, parsley, marjoram, salt, and

pepper to the spinach mixture and blend well. Simmer gently 30 minutes.

A NOTE Serve hot with a sprinkling of freshly grated Parmesan cheese. Keeps in refrigerator for several days or in freezer several months.

ONION SOUP
Serves 6

Only homemade onion soup can approach the aroma and taste of *le vrai soupe à l'oignon.*

4 tablespoons butter
4 large onions, thinly sliced
2 tablespoons flour
6 cups beef stock
½ cup dry white wine
1 teaspoon meat extract
Salt
Pepper

1. In a large heavy skillet, melt the butter and sauté the onion slices slowly until they are golden.
2. Sprinkle the onions with the flour and blend well. Continue to simmer 5 more minutes. Slowly add the stock, wine, and meat extract and continue cooking 45 minutes.
3. Add salt and pepper to taste.

A NOTE Garnish with slices of toasted French bread and freshly grated Parmesan cheese.

SPLIT PEA SOUP
Serves 8

Split peas and ham traditionally combined in a hearty cold-weather soup. Add a loaf of bread and a salad for a one-dish supper.

1 precooked ham shank (2 to 3 pounds), well trimmed
2 cups split peas (quick-cooking kind)
2 small potatoes, peeled and quartered
2 onions, each studded with 1 clove
2 tablespoons tomato paste
8 cups water
Salt
Pepper

1. Combine all the ingredients in a large soup kettle. Bring to a boil and let simmer 1 hour uncovered, or until the peas are soft and the meat is fork tender.
2. Remove the meat and allow it to cool. Meanwhile process the soup in the blender until smooth and adjust the seasoning to taste.
3. When the meat has cooled, cut it into small cubes and add it to the soup.

A NOTE   Serve piping hot and garnish with croutons. Keeps in refrigerator several days or in freezer several months.

MULLIGATAWNY SOUP
Serves 6 to 8

Mulligatawny is an interesting soup, wedding the exotic flavors of an Indian curry with the sturdy goodness of chicken vegetable soup.

2 chicken breasts
6 cups chicken stock
3 tablespoons butter
1 tablespoon oil
1 cup finely chopped onions
1 cup finely chopped celery
1 carrot, finely chopped
1 small tart apple, peeled, cored, and chopped
1 tablespoon curry powder
2 tablespoons flour
½ cup well-drained tomato pulp
Salt
Pepper
Juice 1 lemon
2 cups boiled rice

1. Poach chicken breasts in stock 30 minutes, or until fork tender. Remove meat, cool, then bone and cut in slivers. Reserve stock.

2. In a large heavy saucepan, heat the butter and oil. Sauté the onions, celery, and carrots until soft. Then add chopped apple and continue cooking 2 minutes.

3. Stir in the curry powder and flour and cook until lightly browned.

4. Gradually add chicken stock, stirring constantly. When mixture is smooth, add the tomatoes, salt, and pepper and simmer for 1 hour.

5. Remove from heat and add chicken slivers, lemon juice, and rice.

A NOTE   Serve piping hot, garnished with a sprinkling of finely chopped fresh parsley or thin lemon slices.

CHICKEN-IN-THE-POT
Serves 6 to 8

This was traditional Friday-night fare at Grandmother's, and our favorite gift for a sick friend.

2 chickens (3 pounds each), cut in serving pieces
1 large onion, studded with 3 cloves
4 carrots, thinly sliced
1 whole bunch celery tops, tied together
1 bay leaf
1 small bunch parsley, tied together
¼ teaspoon saffron
Salt
Pepper
½ pound fine egg noodles, cooked

1. In a large heavy pot, place the chicken, onion, carrots, celery, bay leaf, parsley, saffron, salt, and pepper,

and add enough water to cover. Bring to a boil and simmer for 45 minutes.

2. Remove the cooked chicken pieces from the soup and set aside to cool. Remove and discard the onions, celery, parsley, bay leaf, and surface fat.

3. Boil briskly uncovered to reduce liquid in pot to 2 quarts and adjust seasoning to taste.

4. Remove skin and bones from cooled chicken and discard. Cut meat into large pieces, if desired.

5. Add chicken and cooked noodles to soup.

A NOTE Heat and serve with a garnish of chopped fresh parsley.

PIEDMONT MINESTRONE
Serves 6 to 8

Easy to prepare, this hearty dinner soup is an adaptation of a traditional northern Italian favorite.

$\frac{1}{4}$ cup oil
2 pounds beef stew meat, cut in $\frac{1}{2}$-inch cubes
1 can (10$\frac{1}{2}$ ounces) condensed onion soup
5 cups water
1 can (6 ounces) tomato paste
1 tablespoon dried basil
1$\frac{1}{2}$ teaspoons salt
$\frac{1}{4}$ teaspoon pepper
8 carrots, sliced
2 cups sliced celery
1 can (16 ounces) yellow wax beans, drained
1 can (16 ounces) kidney beans, drained

1. In a large heavy saucepan, heat the oil and brown the meat on all sides. Reduce heat to medium and add the undiluted onion soup, water, tomato paste, basil, salt, and pepper. Simmer 1½ hours, covered.

2. Add the carrots, celery, yellow wax beans, and kidney beans. Bring to a boil and simmer 30 minutes, or until tender.

A NOTE   Heat the soup to piping hot and stir in 1 cup freshly grated Parmesan cheese before serving. Keeps in refrigerator several days or freezer several months.

VICHYSSOISE
Serves 6 to 8

Vichyssoise was originated many years ago at a New York hotel by the great chef Louis Diat. Here is a simplified recipe for you to prepare at home.

2 cups peeled and cubed potatoes
2 cups sliced leeks (white part only)
Salt
Pepper
4 cups chicken stock
1 cup heavy cream

1. In large heavy saucepan over medium heat, cook potatoes, leeks, salt, and pepper in chicken stock until tender. Let cool.

2. Process the cooled mixture in the blender until smooth.

3. Refrigerate the soup several hours. When thoroughly chilled, stir in the heavy cream.

A NOTE Serve cold, garnished with a sprinkling of minced chives and freshly grated nutmeg.

GAZPACHO
Serves 6

Gazpacho is delightful summer fare, a liquid salad from Spain. *Olé!*

1 medium cucumber, peeled, seeded, and chopped
1 small green pepper, chopped
1 medium onion, chopped
4 large ripe tomatoes, peeled, quartered, and seeded
2 cloves garlic, split
2 ribs celery, chopped
3 cups tomato juice
2 tablespoons olive oil
1 tablespoon wine vinegar
1 teaspoon dried basil
Salt
Pepper
Dash Tabasco sauce
Juice ½ lemon

1. Process all the ingredients in a blender or food mill in small batches until smooth.
2. Correct the seasoning.
3. Refrigerate overnight to ripen flavors.

A NOTE   Serve well chilled, garnished with garlic croutons and accompanied by small bowls of chopped pepper, cucumber, and tomatoes. Keeps in the refrigerator up to a week.

ORANGE SOUP
Serves 4 to 6

This tomato-based orange soup is not too sweet, and a cooling start to a hot-weather meal.

1 can (28 ounces) peeled tomatoes
1 can (10½ ounces) bouillon
1 can (10½ ounces) water
1 onion, finely chopped
1 tablespoon minced fresh parsley
1 teaspoon sugar
½ teaspoon celery salt
½ cup orange juice
½ cup pitted and deveined orange sections

1. In a heavy saucepan, simmer the tomatoes, bouillon, water, onion, parsley, sugar, and celery salt for 15 minutes.
2. Strain and cool, then process in food mill.
3. Add orange juice and orange sections.

A NOTE   Serve well chilled and garnish each soup bowl with the orange sections. Keeps in refrigerator for several days.

PLUM SOUP
Serves 6

In Scandinavian countries sweet fruit soups such as this one are often served as dessert. American taste generally dictates chilled soup as a first course of a summertime dinner or luncheon menu.

4 cups sliced fresh plums
2 cups water
¼ teaspoon salt
½ cup sugar
Juice 1 lemon
1 cup orange juice
Grated rind 1 lemon
6 orange slices

1. Place plums, water, salt, and sugar in a heavy saucepan. Cover and cook over medium heat until fruit is tender, about 10 minutes.
2. Put mixture through a sieve or food mill.
3. Stir in lemon juice, orange juice, and lemon rind, and chill. Add orange slices.

A NOTE   Serve this hot-weather soup well chilled, and garnish each serving with one of the orange slices. Keeps in refrigerator for several days.

5

The Bread Basket

PROBABLY NO OTHER FOOD symbolizes the hospitality of
home and the warmth of family life more than bread
does. According to old tradition, on baking day the lady
of the house put aside an extra loaf or two for neighbors.
Today, when homemade bread tastes better than ever,
and is surely easier to make, the gift of a crusty loaf fresh
from your oven may renew this gracious custom.

Breads, tea loaves, coffee cakes, muffins, and rolls come

in all sizes and shapes, so gift packaging them suggests some versatility of containers. Quick to come to mind are straw baskets of all shapes and sizes, lacquer plates, wood trays. And for variety:

Tie a gaily printed bandanna hobo-style around a long thin loaf of bread.

Pack a pair of rectangular-shaped loaves into a box for fishing gear.

Crown a circular straw tray or wooden cheese board with a hearty country cheese loaf.

Stand up bread sticks and twists in an executive size pencil holder, majolica mug, ironstone pitcher; or lay them out in a decorative box.

Heap muffins and rolls in a bright colored colander, or a Lucite punch bowl. For children, pack them in a bright red fireman's hat. If you don't deliver your gift bread on baking day, seal it in a plastic bag and freeze it for maximum freshness.

SALLY LUNN BREAD
Makes one 9-inch tube pan

Sally Lunn bread comes to us from England, bearing the name of the young lady who made it popular. You might want to offer this light, sweet ring as did the writer Thackeray—for a meal of "green tea, scandal, hot Sally Lunns and a little novel reading."

1 cup milk
1 package yeast
¼ cup warm water
⅓ cup light brown sugar
½ cup butter, softened
1 teaspoon salt
3 eggs, at room temperature
4 cups flour, sifted

1. Butter a 9-inch tube pan.
2. Scald the milk and let cool to lukewarm.
3. Dissolve the yeast in the water.
4. In a large bowl, cream the sugar, butter, and salt, then beat in the eggs one at a time and add the milk and yeast.
5. Add the flour 1 cup at a time, thoroughly beating the dough until it comes away from the sides of the bowl. Cover with a dish towel and let rise until double in bulk, about an hour.
6. Punch dough down, and place in baking pan. Cover and let rise again until double in bulk.
7. Preheat oven to 375 degrees F.
8. Bake bread for 35 minutes, or until done.

A NOTE Slice Sally Lunn thin and spread it with

whipped butter or orange marmalade for afternoon tea, or in heartier slices with dinner.

COUNTRY CHEESE BREAD
Makes 2 loaves

1½ cups milk, scalded
2 tablespoons sugar
1 tablespoon salt
¼ cup butter, melted
1 teaspoon seasoned pepper
6 to 7 cups all-purpose flour, sifted
7 ounces sharp Cheddar cheese, shredded
2 packages yeast
1 cup lukewarm water
1 egg yolk, lightly beaten with 1 teaspoon water for glaze

1. Butter two 9×5-inch loaf pans.
2. In a large bowl, combine the scalded milk, sugar, salt, butter, and pepper. Set aside to cool.
3. Blend in 2 cups of the flour and beat until smooth. Add the cheese.
4. Dissolve the yeast in the lukewarm water, then add to the milk-cheese mixture, blending in enough of the remaining flour for a soft dough, and mixing until it comes away from the sides of the bowl.
5. Turn dough out on a lightly floured board and knead for about 10 minutes, or until the dough is smooth and elastic.
6. Place dough in a buttered bowl, turning it so it is well coated on all sides. Cover with a dish towel and let rise in a warm place for about an hour, or until double in bulk.

7. Punch dough down, then turn out again on a lightly floured board and knead lightly. Divide the dough in two parts. Shape them into loaves and place them in the prepared pans. Cover and let them rise again for about an hour, or until double in bulk.

8. Preheat oven to 400 degrees F.

9. Paint loaves with beaten egg yolk for a glaze.

10. Bake for 30 to 40 minutes, or until loaves are golden brown. To cool, remove from pan. Loaves should sound hollow when thumped on the bottom crust.

A NOTE Toasting brings forth the full cheese flavor. Serve the bread well buttered, with your favorite soups.

SAVORY HERB BREAD
Makes 2 large loaves

Some breads are rarely made commercially and only come to life in home kitchens. This crusty white loaf, delicately seasoned with fragrant herbs, is one of them.

3 cups lukewarm water
2½ tablespoons sugar
2 packages yeast
2 teaspoons seasoned salt
7½ to 8 cups flour
1 teaspoon dried thyme
1 teaspoon dried basil
1 teaspoon dried marjoram
1 teaspoon grated lemon rind
½ cup butter, softened
1 egg yolk, lightly beaten with 1 teaspoon water for glaze

1. Butter two 9×5-inch loaf pans.
2. Combine ½ cup of the lukewarm water, 1 teaspoon

of the sugar, and the yeast, and let stand in a warm place until the mixture bubbles.

3. In a large bowl, dissolve the seasoned salt in the remaining 2½ cups of water, then add the rest of the sugar and 3 cups of the flour. Mix well.

4. Add the yeast mixture and beat until well combined.

5. Add the thyme, basil, marjoram, lemon rind, and the softened butter, then 4 cups of flour, mixing the dough until it comes away from the sides of the bowl. Let it rest 10 minutes.

6. Sprinkle ½ cup of flour on a pastry board and turn dough out, kneading it thoroughly for about 10 minutes. Use more flour if necessary to make the dough smooth and elastic.

7. Butter the sides of the large bowl and transfer the dough back to it, turning dough so it is coated on all sides. Cover with a dish towel and let rise in warm place for about 1 hour, or until double in bulk.

8. Punch dough down and turn it out on a floured board, kneading it briefly. Divide it in half and shape each portion into a loaf. Place in buttered loaf pans, cover, and let rise in a warm place for another hour, or until dough doubles in bulk and comes up to the tops of the pans.

9. Preheat oven to 350 degrees F.

10. Paint the loaves with the egg yolk glaze.

11. Bake for about 50 minutes, or until loaves are golden brown. Remove from pan. Loaves should sound hollow when thumped on the bottom crust.

A NOTE   A superb sandwich bread, especially agreeable with chicken and roast beef, or in tea sandwiches.

DILLY ONION BREAD
Makes 2 large loaves or 3 small rounds

Most people have never tasted this unusual bread made with cottage cheese. It's highly flavored, crusty yet moist. Surprise a friend who enjoys interesting breads.

2 packages yeast
½ cup warm water
2 cups small curd cottage cheese, at room temperature
¼ cup sugar
2 tablespoons dry minced onions soaked in 1 tablespoon
    water
3 tablespoons butter, melted
½ cup finely chopped fresh dill sprigs or 2 tablespoons
    dried dill weed, rubbed fine
2 teaspoons salt
½ teaspoon baking soda
2 eggs, at room temperature, lightly beaten
6 to 7 cups flour
1 egg, lightly beaten with 1 tablespoon water for glaze

1. Butter two 9×5-inch loaf pans or three 8-inch round pans.
2. Dissolve yeast in the warm water.
3. In a large bowl, mix cheese, sugar, onion, and butter together. Then add dill, salt, soda, eggs, and yeast mixture.
4. Add enough flour to make dough stiff and mix thoroughly until it comes away from the sides of the bowl.

5. Turn dough out on floured board and knead 10 minutes.

6. Place dough in buttered bowl and turn to coat on all sides. Cover with a dish towel and let rise in a warm place for 1 hour, or until double in bulk.

7. Punch dough down and knead lightly on a floured board. Shape and put into the prepared pans.

8. Preheat oven to 375 degrees F.

9. Paint loaves with egg glaze.

10. Bake about 45 minutes, or until golden.

A NOTE   This belongs in your bread basket when serving tuna, salmon, shrimp, cucumber, and egg salads.

SEEDED EGG TWIST, OR CHALLAH
Makes 3 large loaves

2 packages yeast
2½ cups warm water
6 tablespoons sugar
2 teaspoons salt
⅓ cup salad oil
5 eggs, at room temperature
9 cups all-purpose unbleached flour
1 egg yolk, lightly beaten with 1 teaspoon cold water for
        glaze
3 tablespoons poppy seeds

1. Butter three 9×5-inch loaf pans.

2. In a large bowl, dissolve the yeast in the warm water.

3. Add the sugar, salt, oil, eggs, and 4 cups of the flour. Beat vigorously, gradually adding more flour until the dough comes away from the sides of the bowl.

4. Spread remaining flour on a board, turn dough out on it, and knead until dough is smooth and elastic, and the flour is absorbed. If the dough is still sticky after using all the flour, add more, a little at a time, until you get the right consistency for easy handling.

5. Return dough to large bowl, cover with a dish towel, and let it rise in a warm place for 1 to 3 hours, or until it triples in bulk.

6. Punch dough down and divide it into nine equal pieces. On a lightly floured board, shape each piece into a rope about 1½ inches in diameter.

7. Braid three ropes at a time, each set forming one loaf. At the end of each loaf pinch the ropes together. Place loaves in individual baking pans and set in a warm place to rise for 45 minutes, or until double in bulk.

8. Preheat oven to 375 degrees F.

9. Paint tops of loaves with the egg yolk glaze, and sprinkle with poppy seeds.

10. Bake in preheated oven 30 to 40 minutes, or until the breads are golden. Cool on a rack.

A NOTE   Enjoy!

CONTINENTAL BAGUETTES
Makes 2 loaves

While nothing can reproduce the crusty French bread of
your travels, here is a reasonable facsimile, adapted for
the limitations of American house ovens.

1 package yeast
1 tablespoon sugar
1½ cups warm water
2 teaspoons salt
4 cups all-purpose unbleached flour
1 egg white, lightly beaten with 1 tablespoon water for
    glaze

1. Butter a large baking sheet, then dust it with corn
meal.
2. In a large bowl, dissolve the yeast and sugar in ½
cup of the warm water, then add remaining water, salt,
and 3 cups of the flour. Beat with a wooden spoon until
the dough comes away from the sides of the bowl.
3. Turn dough out on a floured board and add remaining cup of flour. Knead until the dough is smooth and
elastic and all the flour has been absorbed. Cover with a
dish towel and set in a warm place for an hour, or until
the dough has doubled in bulk.
4. Punch dough down, then cover and let rise again for
45 minutes.
5. Divide the dough in half, shape each portion into a
long thin loaf or baguette, and place on prepared baking
sheet. On the top of each loaf cut four shallow slanted

slits with a sharp knife, and let the loaves rise for another half hour, or until double in bulk.

6. Preheat oven to 400 degrees F.

7. Brush tops of loaves with the egg white glaze.

8. Place a shallow pan of boiling water on the lowest shelf in the oven and bake the loaves in preheated oven for 45 minutes, or until they are golden and sound hollow when thumped on the crust.

9. Cool on a rack.

A NOTE Crunchy and crusty alone, and spectacular spread with herb or garlic butter.

ANADAMA RAISIN BREAD
Makes 2 loaves

Anadama bread is said to come from the shores of Massachusetts where a legendary Gloucester fisherman became annoyed because his wife fed him only corn meal and molasses. One night, in a fit of anger, he mixed them together with yeast and flour and threw the whole mess at the fireplace, crying, "Anna, damn her!" An apocryphal story, perhaps, but an excellent bread nevertheless.

4 to 5 cups flour
1 cup corn meal
2 packages yeast
1 tablespoon salt
½ cup raisins
¼ cup cinnamon sugar
2 cups hot water
½ cup molasses
5 tablespoons butter, softened

1. Butter two 9×5-inch loaf pans.

2. In a large bowl, combine 4 cups of the flour, the corn meal, yeast, salt, and raisins tossed in cinnamon sugar.

3. In another bowl, combine the water, molasses, and butter. Add this to the flour mixture and beat well with a wooden spoon until it is fairly soft and not too sticky.

4. Turn dough out on a floured board and knead it for 10 minutes, or until it is easily handled and no longer sticky. You may have to add up to a cup of additional flour.

5. Place dough in buttered bowl and turn it so it is well coated on all sides. Cover with dish towel and let it rise in a warm place for about 2 hours, or until double in bulk.

6. Punch dough down and turn it out on floured board. Divide it into two equal portions, shaping each into a loaf. Place in prepared pans and let rise for 1 hour in a warm place, or until double in bulk.

7. Preheat oven to 375 degrees F.

8. Bake the loaves for 40 to 50 minutes, or until they are browned. Remove from pans. Loaves should sound hollow when thumped on the crust.

9. Cool on a rack.

A NOTE   This makes especially good toast; serve it with morning coffee or afternoon tea.

SWEDISH RYE
Makes 2 oblong loaves

What makes this Swedish rye distinctive is the touch of orange rind.

1 cup milk
2 teaspoons salt
3 tablespoons molasses
2 tablespoons butter, softened
1 package yeast
1 cup warm water
3½ cups white flour, sifted
2 tablespoons caraway seeds
2 tablespoons grated orange rind
2 cups rye flour

1. Butter a baking sheet and dust with corn meal.

2. Scald milk and pour over the salt, molasses, and butter. Let cool.

3. Dissolve the yeast in the warm water and add to cooled milk mixture.

4. Stir in the white flour and beat until smooth.

5. Combine the caraway seeds, orange rind, and rye flour and add gradually, mixing until the dough is fairly stiff. Turn it out on a floured board and knead it for about 10 minutes, or until smooth and elastic.

6. Transfer the dough to a buttered bowl, turning it so it is well coated on all sides. Cover with a dish towel and let rise in a warm place for about 2 hours, or until double in bulk.

7. Punch dough down, cover it, and let rise again until double in bulk.

8. Turn dough out on floured board and shape it into two oblong loaves. Place them on prepared baking sheet. Cover and let them rise again until double in bulk.

9. Preheat oven to 375 degrees F.

10. Bake loaves for 40 minutes.

A NOTE Open-faced sandwiches, breakfast toast, picnic fare.

AUTHENTIC CORNELL BREAD
Makes 2 loaves

Experiments conducted at the Cornell University School of Nutrition proved that man can indeed live by bread alone—using the Triple Rich Formula. This health bread formula adds a minimum of 1 tablespoon of soy flour, 1 tablespoon of skim milk powder, and 1 teaspoon of wheat germ to the bottom of each cup of flour. You can delight health food fans by incorporating this formula in any bread, cake, or cookie recipe, but start with this classic bread.

3 cups warm water
2 packages yeast
2 tablespoons honey
6 to 7 cups flour
3 tablespoons wheat germ
½ cup full-fat soy flour
¾ cup skim milk powder
4 teaspoons salt
2 tablespoons salad oil

1. Grease two 9×5-inch loaf pans.
2. In a large bowl, combine the water, yeast, and honey and let stand for 10 minutes.
3. Sift together 6 cups of the flour, wheat germ, soy flour, and skim milk powder.
4. Stir the yeast mixture, gradually adding the salt and 3 cups of the flour mixture. Beat vigorously.
5. Stir in the salad oil and 3 more cups of flour mixture, then turn out on a floured board and add remaining flour mixture. Knead for 10 minutes, or until dough

is smooth and elastic, adding additional flour if needed for easy handling.

6. Place dough in a buttered bowl and turn so all sides are coated, then cover with dish towel and let rise in a warm place for an hour, or until double in bulk.

7. Punch dough down in bowl and let rise another 15 minutes.

8. Turn out on floured board, shape into two loaves, and place in loaf pans. Cover and let rise for 45 minutes, or until double in bulk.

9. Preheat oven to 350 degrees F.

10. Bake for 50 to 60 minutes. If loaves start to brown too quickly (in 15 to 20 minutes), turn oven down to 325 degrees F.

A NOTE A generally useful, highly nutritious white bread, great for the lunch pail.

EASY BRIOCHE
Makes 24 individual or 2 large brioches

Typically French, brioche is said to come from the district of Brie, where it is served warm for breakfast. In America, we enjoy this golden bread at any time of day.

½ cup milk
1 package yeast
¼ cup warm water
½ cup butter, softened
⅓ cup sugar
1 teaspoon salt
4 eggs, at room temperature
4 cups flour, sifted
1 egg, lightly beaten with 1 tablespoon water for glaze

1. Scald milk and set aside to cool to lukewarm.

2. Dissolve yeast in the warm water.

3. In a large bowl, cream the butter and gradually add the sugar and salt, creaming the ingredients together.

4. To the creamed mixture, add the dissolved yeast, lukewarm milk, eggs, and flour.

5. Beat the dough for 2 minutes, then cover with dish towel and let rise in a warm place for about 2 hours or until double in bulk.

6. Punch dough down and beat for 2 minutes. Then cover tightly with aluminum foil and refrigerate overnight.

7. Let dough come to room temperature.

8. Preheat oven to 375 degrees F. and butter 24 individual or 2 large fluted brioche pans. If unavailable, substitute muffin tins for individual brioches and 1-pound coffee cans for large brioches.

9. When brioche dough is at room temperature, punch it down again and turn out on a lightly floured board.

10. For individual brioches, divide dough into two parts, one consisting of three fourths of the total dough, the other part the remaining quarter. Divide the larger portion into twenty-four equal pieces, form into smooth balls, and put them in the prepared muffin tins. Cut the smaller section into twenty-four equal pieces and form them into balls to make the brioche topknots. Make a dent in the center of each large ball, wet slightly with cold water, and press a small ball into the dent.

11. For large brioches, divide the dough into two parts, one consisting of three fourths of the total dough, the other part the remaining quarter. Divide the larger portion in half, form each half into a smooth ball, and place in the prepared brioche pans. Divide the smaller portion

of dough into two balls. Make a dent in the center of each large ball, wet slightly with cold water, and press a small ball into the dent to form the topknot.

12. Let brioches rise in a warm place, covered, for about an hour, or until double in bulk.

13. Glaze brioches with the beaten egg and bake individual brioches 15 to 20 minutes and large brioches 30 to 35 minutes. Cool on a cake rack and keep in plastic bag, tightly closed.

A NOTE   Reheat brioches at 250 degrees F. for 10 minutes, and serve with whipped butter and strawberry jam.

PARMESAN CHEESE TWISTS
Makes 32 sticks

6 tablespoons milk
1 package yeast
½ cup warm water
1 tablespoon butter, melted
1 teaspoon sugar
½ teaspoon salt
½ cup freshly grated Parmesan cheese
2 to 3 cups all-purpose flour
1 egg white, lightly beaten with 1 tablespoon water for
     glaze
Paprika

1. Grease two cookie sheets.
2. Scald milk and set aside to cool.

3. Dissolve yeast in the warm water.

4. In a large bowl, combine scalded milk, butter, sugar, salt, and cheese. Add dissolved yeast and 2 cups of the flour. Stir until the dough is smooth and comes away from the sides of the bowl.

5. Sprinkle ½ cup of flour on a pastry board and turn dough out on it. Knead until all the flour has been incorporated and the dough is smooth and elastic. If needed, work in remaining ½ cup of flour.

6. Put dough in a large bowl, cover with dish towel, and let rise in a warm place for 1 hour or until double in bulk.

7. Roll dough out to ½-inch thickness. Cut it into 32 strips 5 inches long. Twist the strips loosely and place on prepared cookie sheets. Cover and let rise until twists are double in bulk.

8. Preheat oven to 425 degrees F.

9. Brush tops of cheese twists with egg white glaze and sprinkle lightly with paprika.

10. Bake for 15 minutes.

A NOTE   Keep cheese twists crisp and dry in an airtight container, and serve with cocktails, soup, or salad.

APPLESAUCE MUFFINS
Makes 16 muffins

Muffins for breakfast were a wonderful old custom and worthy of reviving. Our candidate is this fragrant and spicy applesauce muffin.

2 cups all-purpose flour, sifted
¼ cup sugar
3 teaspoons double-acting baking powder
½ teaspoon salt
1 teaspoon allspice
2 large eggs, beaten
1 cup milk
½ cup applesauce
¼ cup shortening, melted
½ cup white raisins

1. Preheat oven to 400 degrees F. and line muffin pans with paper muffin cups.
2. In a large mixing bowl, sift flour, sugar, baking powder, salt, and allspice.
3. In another bowl, combine eggs, milk, and applesauce and stir into flour mixture. Add melted shortening and raisins.
4. Fill paper muffin cups two thirds full and bake for 30 minutes or until inserted cake tester comes out clean and muffins are golden.

A NOTE   Warm in a 250 degree F. oven for 12 minutes and, for a special breakfast, serve with a dollop of applesauce.

BLUEBERRY MUFFINS
Makes 12 muffins

When blueberries are in season don't miss the opportunity to try these lovely muffins. The crisp lemon sugar topping makes them especially giftworthy.

2 cups packaged regular biscuit mix
½ cup sugar
1 cup sour cream
1 egg
1½ cups fresh blueberries
2 teaspoons grated lemon rind

1. Preheat oven to 425 degrees F. and line muffin pan with paper muffin cups.
2. In a large bowl, combine biscuit mix and ¼ cup of the sugar. Make a well in the center of the dry ingredients, and add the sour cream and egg, stirring with a fork until they are combined.
3. Gently fold in the blueberries.
4. Spoon about ¼ cup of batter into the paper muffin cups, filling no more than two thirds full.
5. In a small bowl, mix the lemon peel and remaining ¼ cup of sugar and sprinkle over the batter in each cup.
6. Bake for 20 to 25 minutes.

A NOTE   Take the chill off the muffins by warming in a 250 degree F. oven for 10 minutes.

BACON CORN STICKS
Makes 14 to 16 corn sticks

Crumbled bacon adds crunch and flavor to an old favorite.

1¼ cups yellow corn meal
¾ cup all-purpose flour, sifted
¼ cup sugar
4 teaspoons baking powder
½ teaspoon salt
2 eggs
1 cup milk
¼ cup shortening, melted
¼ cup crumbled bacon

1. Preheat oven to 425 degrees F.
2. In a large bowl, sift together the corn meal, flour, sugar, baking powder, and salt.
3. Add eggs, milk, and shortening, and beat just until smooth.
4. Stir in the bacon bits.
5. Grease and preheat the corn stick molds in the oven, then pour batter in when pan is sizzling. Bake for 15 to 20 minutes.

A NOTE Dress up cold suppers with a basket of corn sticks, warmed for 10 minutes in a 250 degree F. oven.

SCONES
Makes 16 rounds

Sounding very much like they belong in a drawing room comedy, scones are really traditional fare in English country houses. They are simple and lovely tea biscuits, easy to make and smashing to serve.

2 cups flour
½ teaspoon salt
2½ teaspoons double-acting baking powder
¼ cup sugar
½ cup shortening
½ cup currants
2 eggs, and enough milk to make ⅔ cup liquid

1. Preheat oven to 425 degrees F. and butter a cookie sheet.
2. In a large mixing bowl, combine the flour, salt, baking powder, and sugar. Cut in shortening with two knives and add the currants. Add the egg mixture and stir until mixed.
3. Place dough on floured board and knead lightly for a few minutes. Roll dough out ¼ inch thick and cut into rounds with a fluted cookie cutter.
4. Place scones 1½ inches apart on prepared cookie sheet and bake for 15 minutes, or until golden.

A NOTE   Heat scones for 15 minutes or less in a 300 degree F. oven. Enjoy them split and spread lavishly with butter.

6

Dinner in a Dish

ALL-IN-ONE-DISH MEALS make particularly felicitous gifts, so consider them for a busy hostess, a sick friend, or anyone short of time and long on mouths to feed. This chapter offers recipes for chicken, veal, beef, lamb, pork, and seafood dishes, and a few cold salads that are fun for picnics or hot-weather meals. Many of them are better made a day or two ahead, and all but the salads can be frozen.

For best results, give some dinners in the same reheat-

able containers in which you made—for instance, chicken
crêpes Florentine, chicken potpie, lasagna, moussaka, and
shrimp Aegean. Select your containers carefully before
preparing these dishes; consider prettily decorated baking dishes or, more frugally, aluminum foil pans of proper
size which can be nestled in straw or plastic trays.

The remaining recipes can be packaged with more versatility. Remember to line containers with foil, plastic
wrap or a plastic bag. For example:

Heap Viennese goulash in a sparkling glass pitcher,
and any of the stews in an ice bucket.

Pack chicken Orientale or chicken Basque in a clear
plastic planter.

Pile stuffed cabbage or chili in a paper paint pail and
tie with a gay checked napkin.

Pack turkey Tetrazzini or meatballs in plastic bags
and pack in a lunch pail, tying on a package of thin spaghetti if desired.

Place slices of vitello tonnato or pot roast in a fish bowl
and spoon their sauces over.

Arrange any of the salads prettily in a Wok.

TURKEY TETRAZZINI
Serves 24

This dish was named in honor of Luisa Tetrazzini, a famous coloratura soprano, who probably never even tasted it. This triple recipe is eminently suitable for a church supper or community fair.

3 turkey breasts (about 5 pounds each)
1 package soup greens
2 tablespoons salt
½ pound butter
1½ cups flour
5 teaspoons salt
½ teaspoon pepper
½ teaspoon nutmeg
3 cups heavy cream
⅓ cup medium dry sherry
1½ cups freshly grated Parmesan cheese
1½ pounds mushrooms, sliced
Juice ½ lemon

1. In a large pot, cover turkey breasts with water, add soup greens and salt, and cook until just tender, about 2½ to 3 hours.

2. Remove turkey from stock and set aside to cool. Skim excess fat from stock.

3. Boil stock briskly until it is reduced to 8 cups. Strain and discard vegetables.

4. In a heavy 5-quart saucepan, melt ¼ pound of the butter. Remove from heat and stir in the flour to form a paste. Return pan to heat and let mixture bubble for 2 minutes, stirring constantly.

5. Gradually add the strained stock, stirring over medium high heat until sauce comes to a boil and thickens. Remove from heat, and season with salt, pepper, and nutmeg. Stir in the heavy cream, sherry, and cheese, and set aside.

6. Sauté the sliced mushrooms in the remaining butter. Sprinkle with lemon juice and add to the cream sauce.

7. Cut or pull apart the turkey breasts into inch-wide slivers of meat, and mix with the cream sauce.

A NOTE   Cook 1½ pounds of thin spaghetti *al dente,* drain well, and lay in the bottom of two large shallow baking dishes. Pour half the turkey mixture into each dish and sprinkle with ¼ cup grated Parmesan cheese and paprika. Bake 30 to 40 minutes in a preheated 350 degree F. oven.

CHICKEN BASQUE
Serves 6 to 8

A regional French specialty, happily combining chicken, vegetables, and white wine.

½ pound salt pork, diced
2 tablespoons butter
3 small frying chickens, in pieces
3 cups sliced onions
1 cup chopped celery
4 cloves garlic, pressed
1 small eggplant, peeled and coarsely cubed
1 pound mushrooms, sliced

3 cups drained canned Italian-style tomatoes
1 cup dry white wine
Salt
Pepper
1 teaspoon dried basil
1 teaspoon dried thyme

1. Preheat oven to 350 degrees F.
2. Sauté the salt pork in the butter until golden. Remove from the pan with a slotted spoon, drain on absorbent paper and set aside.
3. Brown the chicken pieces in the same pan. Remove them to a large ovenproof casserole.
4. In the same pan, sauté the onions, celery, and garlic until wilted, then add to the casserole.
5. Lightly sauté the eggplant cubes and mushrooms in the same pan and add them to the casserole.
6. To the casserole, add the tomatoes and white wine, and season with salt, pepper, basil, and thyme.
7. Bake casserole for 45 minutes.
8. Sprinkle cooked pork bits on top.

A NOTE Bake in a preheated 350 degree F. oven for 30 minutes, or until thoroughly heated. Garnish with chopped fresh parsley.

CHICKEN ORIENTALE
Serves 4

This chicken dish is sweet and tangy, and delightfully easy to prepare.

2 broilers, cut up
4 tablespoons butter
¼ cup soy sauce
1 clove garlic, minced
½ cup red currant jelly
1 tablespoon Dijon mustard
1 cup orange juice
1 teaspoon powdered ginger
1 teaspoon powdered coriander

1. Pat broilers dry and put them in a shallow baking dish.

2. In a saucepan, melt the butter, then add the remaining ingredients, stirring until the jelly is melted and the sauce is smooth. Cool.

3. Pour the sauce over the chicken and marinate at least 2 to 3 hours.

4. Preheat oven to 350 degrees F.

5. Cover the chicken with foil and bake 45 minutes. Remove foil, raise oven temperature to 400 degrees F., and baste frequently until chicken is brown, about 15 minutes.

A NOTE   Heat dish in preheated 300 degree F. oven about 30 minutes. Serve chicken pieces on a bed of rice and drizzle enough sauce over chicken just to moisten; serve the rest in a sauceboat. Sprinkle chopped dry roasted peanuts over the chicken and garnish the platter with orange slices and chopped parsley.

CHICKEN POTPIE
Serves 4

Here is an all-American favorite with the sophisticated addition of white wine.

1 fowl (4 to 5 pounds)
1 large onion, studded with 4 cloves
1 bunch celery leaves, tied together
1 bunch parsley, tied together
Salt
Pepper
4 tablespoons butter
4 tablespoons flour
½ cup dry white wine
½ cup heavy cream
1 tablespoon lemon juice
Pinch freshly grated nutmeg
1 box (10 ounces) frozen mixed vegetables, cooked and
    drained
1 top piecrust, cut to fit top of serving dish, vented and
    baked flat on a cookie sheet.

1. Place the chicken, onion, celery, parsley, salt, and pepper in a large heavy saucepan and almost cover with water. Let simmer about 1½ hours, or until chicken is tender but still firm.

2. Remove chicken from stock and set aside until cool enough to handle. Skim off excess fat from stock.

3. Boil the stock until it is reduced to 1½ cups. Discard vegetables and let stock cool.

4. Melt the butter in a heavy saucepan, stir in the flour to make a smooth paste, and cook 2 minutes. Gradually add the stock, stirring constantly to prevent lumps. Cook, stirring, until mixture thickens. Add the wine, cream, lemon juice, nutmeg, and additional salt and pepper to taste.

5. Cut the cooled chicken into bite-size pieces.

6. Combine the chicken and cooked vegetables with the cream sauce, and pour the mixture into a 2-quart baking or soufflé dish.

7. Cover the baking dish with the prebaked piecrust.

A NOTE   Reheat at 325 degrees F. for 30 minutes.

CHICKEN CRÊPES FLORENTINE
Makes about 14 crêpes

Elegant and inexpensive, this is a happy culinary marriage of favorite foods—chicken, spinach, cheese sauce, crêpes.

Crêpes
1 egg
1 cup milk
⅔ cup flour
2 tablespoons butter, melted
Salt

3 packages (10 ounces) frozen spinach or 2 pounds fresh
     spinach
4 tablespoons butter, melted
4 tablespoons flour

2 cups milk
1 cup heavy cream
Freshly grated nutmeg
Salt
Pepper
1 cup grated Swiss cheese
3 cups cooked chopped chicken meat
1 cup cooked chopped ham
½ cup freshly grated Parmesan cheese

1. Beat egg and milk together in a bowl.
2. Add flour, melted butter, and salt and continue beating until batter is smooth.
3. Heat a lightly buttered crêpe pan and, using about 2 tablespoons of batter at a time, cook the crêpes until light golden brown on both sides. Set crêpes aside.
4. Butter a shallow 1½-quart baking dish.
5. Cook the spinach and drain thoroughly. Spread evenly over the bottom of the baking dish.
6. In a saucepan, combine the melted butter and flour, stirring constantly over medium heat. Gradually add the milk and cream. When the sauce is thick, add the nutmeg, salt, and pepper and remove from the heat. Stir in the grated Swiss cheese and mix well.
7. Combine the chicken and ham with ¾ cup of the cream sauce.
8. Spoon 2 tablespoons of the meat mixture in the center of each crêpe and roll. Arrange the filled crêpes close together on top of the spinach in the baking dish.
9. Pour the remaining sauce over the crêpes and sprinkle the top with Parmesan cheese.

A NOTE Preheat oven to 350 degrees F. and bake for 30 minutes, or until thoroughly heated.

SAVORY POT ROAST
Serves 6 to 8

This family recipe from a dear friend incorporates an interesting way of making gravy from cooked bread crusts.

3 cloves garlic
Salt
Pepper
Paprika
Worcestershire sauce
1 rump or round roast of beef (4 pounds)
¼ cup wine vinegar
4 large onions, sliced
½ cup oil
3 cups beef stock
1 cup red wine
1 bay leaf
1 heel of rye bread or crusts from 4 slices

1. In a small bowl, press garlic and make a paste with the salt, pepper, paprika, and Worcestershire sauce. Rub meat with mixture.

2. Place seasoned meat in a large bowl and sprinkle it with the wine vinegar. Cover and refrigerate several hours or overnight.

3. Remove meat from refrigerator and let stand at room temperature. Dry meat thoroughly.

4. In a Dutch oven, brown the sliced onions in oil. Remove onions with slotted spoon and set aside.

5. In the same pot, brown the meat well on all sides. Add the browned onions, beef stock, red wine, bay leaf, bread crusts, and cook, covered, on top of stove, about 3 hours or until meat is tender.

6. Remove meat and set aside. Discard bay leaf and skim excess fat from cooking liquid. Then put liquid, onions, and bread crusts in blender and process to make gravy.

7. Trim meat and slice when completely cool and cover with gravy.

A NOTE   Preheat oven to 350 degrees F. and bake for 45 minutes, or until meat is thoroughly heated. Serve with buttered noodles or parsley potatoes and pass extra gravy in a sauceboat if desired.

VIENNESE GOULASH
Serves 6 to 8

This is an authentic goulash, the next best thing to an Austrian trip.

2 tablespoons oil
2 tablespoons butter
3 pounds onions, sliced
3 cloves garlic, chopped
1 tablespoon dried marjoram
2 tablespoons paprika
2 teaspoons finely crushed caraway seeds
Grated rind 1 small lemon
4 pounds beef, cut into small cubes and lightly floured
1 can (10½ ounces) beef bouillon, plus enough water to
    make 2 cups
2 tablespoons tomato paste
1 bay leaf
Salt
Pepper

1. In a large heavy skillet, heat the oil and butter and sauté the onions and garlic until golden. Stir in the marjoram, paprika, caraway seeds, and lemon rind. Remove mixture to a large casserole.

2. In the same pan, brown the lightly floured beef cubes a few at a time, adding more oil if needed. Transfer the browned meat to the large casserole.

3. Mix the bouillon and water with the tomato paste and add to the casserole. Season with bay leaf, salt, and pepper.

4. Cover the casserole tightly and let the goulash cook slowly for 3 hours, or until the meat is tender.

5. If desired, thicken the sauce with additional flour.

A NOTE Reheat thoroughly on range over low heat. This Viennese specialty is traditionally served with buttered noodles.

BEEF STEW NEAPOLITAN
Serves 8

6 tablespoons oil
4 medium onions, coarsely chopped
2 cups coarsely chopped celery
1 green pepper, coarsely chopped
3 cloves garlic, chopped
2 large cans (28 ounces each) Italian-style tomatoes
¼ cup finely chopped parsley
1 teaspoon dried oregano
2 teaspoons dried basil
1 teaspoon finely crushed dried rosemary

Salt
Pepper
2 tablespoons butter
5 pounds beef, cut in cubes
1 cup white wine

1. In a large heavy saucepan, heat 4 tablespoons of oil and sauté the onions, celery, green pepper, and garlic until golden.

2. Add tomatoes, parsley, oregano, basil, rosemary, salt, and pepper. Simmer uncovered 15 minutes, and set aside.

3. In a heavy skillet, heat the butter and remaining 2 tablespoons of oil and brown the beef cubes a few at a time, adding them to the saucepan as they are browned.

4. Add the white wine to the empty skillet, and bring it to a boil, scraping the bottom of the pan with a wooden spoon. Then pour the white wine into the saucepan and let the stew simmer uncovered for about 2½ hours, or until the meat is tender.

A NOTE Reheat thoroughly on range over low heat and serve with linguine.

CHILI CON CARNE
Serves 4 to 6

A tasty and inexpensive dish adapted from the distinctive cuisine of the American Southwest and Mexico.

4 tablespoons oil
2 onions, chopped
3 cloves garlic, chopped
2 pounds ground round
1 tablespoon salt
1 large can (28 ounces) Italian-style tomatoes
3 tablespoons chili powder
2 teaspoons coriander
1 teaspoon cumin
1 tablespoon dried basil
1 can (16 ounces) red kidney beans, drained

1. In a large heavy frying pan, heat the oil and sauté the onions and garlic until golden. Add meat and stir until browned. Add salt.

2. Discard excess oil and add tomatoes, chili powder, coriander, cumin, and basil. Simmer 2 hours, or until the liquid is absorbed and mixture is thick.

3. Add kidney beans and mix well.

A NOTE   Reheat thoroughly on range over low heat, and serve Mexican-style with tacos.

STUFFED CABBAGE
Serves 6 to 8

While nostalgia for Grandma's cooking sometimes belies the reality, this dish was really Grandma's finest. We present it here with happy childhood memories.

1 large head cabbage
1 cup applesauce
½ cup seedless raisins
Juice 1 small lemon
12 gingersnaps, crushed
2 tablespoons brown sugar
1 can (8 ounces) tomato sauce
2 eggs
2 pounds ground lean chuck
Salt
Pepper

1. Soak cabbage in hot water for 10 minutes, then cut away core. Cook in boiling water for 5 to 10 minutes, or until cabbage leaves are pliant. Remove cabbage from water and drain.

2. Remove the eighteen largest cabbage leaves and set aside.

3. Chop the remaining cabbage leaves coarsely and place in a large cooking pot with the applesauce, raisins, lemon juice, gingersnaps, sugar, and tomato sauce. Combine well.

4. Beat the eggs with a fork and mix thoroughly with the ground beef. Season to taste with salt and pepper.

5. Place a small amount of the meat mixture in the center of each cabbage leaf. Fold the leaf over the meat on all sides, envelope-style, and secure with toothpicks. Place the stuffed cabbage leaves on top of the other ingredients in the pot.

6. Add enough water to the pot almost to cover the stuffed cabbage, bring it to a boil, and then simmer covered for 1½ hours.

A NOTE   Lay the stuffed cabbage, folded side down, in

the bottom of a large shallow baking dish and half cover with sauce. Preheat the oven to 350 degrees F. and heat the meat uncovered for half an hour, or until thoroughly heated and nicely browned. Heat the remaining sauce separately and serve in a sauceboat accompanied by rice.

MEATBALLS IN TOMATO SAUCE
Serves 8

Without question, this is the favorite dinner of every child we know.

½ cup oil
2 onions, chopped
4 cloves garlic, chopped
1 teaspoon anise seeds, crushed
1 tablespoon oregano
4 sweet Italian sausages (½ pound), skins removed
2 teaspoons salt
1 teaspoon pepper
1 bay leaf
2 cans (6 ounces each) tomato paste
2 cans (28 ounces each) Italian-style tomatoes
1 cup water
2 teaspoons sugar
2 pounds ground lean chuck
2 eggs
¼ cup milk
1 cup seasoned bread crumbs
1 tablespoon dried basil
½ cup finely chopped fresh parsley

1. In a heavy 5-quart pot, heat the oil and cook the onions until transparent. Add the garlic, anise seeds, oregano, sausages, salt, pepper, bay leaf, tomato paste, tomatoes, water, and sugar and simmer for 1½ hours.

2. Mix meat, eggs, milk, and bread crumbs together and form into balls. Season to taste with salt and pepper.

3. After the sauce has cooked, add the meatballs and cook 1 hour more without stirring.

4. Add the basil and parsley and simmer for 15 minutes.

A NOTE   Try serving it with some less familiar pastas as well as with spaghetti.

LASAGNA
Serves 8

2 pounds ground lean chuck
4 tablespoons oil
1 cup chopped onions
2 large cloves garlic, chopped
½ pound sweet Italian sausage
1 large can (35 ounces) Italian-style tomatoes
2 cans (6 ounces each) tomato paste
1 cup water
Salt
Pepper
½ teaspoon ground anise
1 tablespoon oregano
1 tablespoon dried basil
¼ teaspoon red pepper

1 pound ricotta cheese
2 eggs, beaten
¼ cup chopped fresh parsley leaves
1 pound lasagna noodles
½ pound shredded mozzarella cheese

1. In a heavy skillet, brown ground meat. Discard excess fat and set meat aside.

2. In a large heavy pot, heat the oil and sauté the onions and garlic until golden.

3. Remove the casing from the Italian sausage and brown in the pot with onions and garlic.

4. Add browned meat to pot and add the tomatoes, tomato paste, water, salt, pepper, anise, oregano, basil, and red pepper. Simmer on the stove uncovered for 3 hours.

5. When the sauce is ready, mix together the ricotta cheese, eggs, parsley, and salt and pepper to taste. Set aside.

6. In a large pot bring 8 quarts of salted water to a boil. Add the lasagna to the boiling water, a few pieces at a time, and cook 10 to 12 minutes, or until *al dente*.

7. Drain the noodles and refill the pot with cold water. Return the lasagna to the cold water and add a few drops of oil to prevent sticking.

8. In a large rectangular baking dish with sides at least 2½ to 3 inches high, spread a little meat sauce. Lay slightly overlapping strips of lasagna on the sauce. Spoon one third of the ricotta mixture over the noodles, then a layer of meat sauce, and finally sprinkle one fourth of the mozzarella cheese. Repeat two more times, ending with a fourth layer of lasagna. Top with meat sauce and mozzarella cheese.

A NOTE Preheat oven to 350 degrees F., cover the lasagna tightly with foil, and bake for 45 to 60 minutes. This dish freezes well but takes a surprisingly long time to defrost (about 24 hours at room temperature).

MOUSSAKA
Serves 8 to 10

This happy combination of lamb and eggplant was originally from Rumania, and is now made in many eastern countries. Our recipe comes from a Greek friend.

2 eggplants (about 1 pound each)
Salt
½ cup oil
5 tablespoons butter
2 onions, finely chopped
1 clove garlic, chopped
2 pounds ground lean lamb
2 cans (6 ounces each) tomato paste
¾ cup water
½ cup dry red wine
¼ cup black coffee
1 teaspoon oregano

1 teaspoon dried rosemary, crushed well
¼ teaspoon cinnamon
Pepper
3 tablespoons flour
2 cups milk
2 egg yolks
¼ teaspoon freshly grated nutmeg
¾ cup freshly grated Parmesan cheese
¾ cup flavored bread crumbs

1 Cut the eggplants into ½-inch slices, sprinkle them with salt, and let stand 20 minutes.

2. Wipe eggplants dry with paper towels, brush them

with oil, and broil the slices until golden brown on both sides. Set aside.

3. In a large skillet, melt 2 tablespoons of the butter and sauté the onions and garlic until golden. Add the lamb and brown. Add the tomato paste, water, wine, coffee, oregano, rosemary, cinnamon, salt, and pepper. Simmer uncovered until most of the liquid is absorbed and the sauce is thick. Set aside.

4. In a heavy saucepan, melt the remaining 3 tablespoons of butter. Remove from heat and add the flour, stirring to form a smooth paste. Return the pan to the heat and slowly add the milk, stirring constantly until the mixture forms a smooth thick cream sauce.

5. Beat the egg yolks in a small bowl, then stir in a little of the hot cream sauce. Add the yolk mixture to the saucepan. Add the nutmeg and season to taste with salt and pepper.

6. In a small bowl, combine the grated Parmesan cheese and bread crumbs and set aside.

7. In a large baking dish, place a layer of eggplant slices and sprinkle with one third of the cheese bread crumbs. Add a layer of meat sauce and sprinkle with another third of the cheese bread crumbs. Add a second layer of sliced eggplant and a second layer of meat sauce. Cover with the cream sauce and cover the top with the remaining third of the cheese bread crumbs.

A NOTE   Preheat oven to 375 degrees F. and bake the moussaka for 45 minutes, or until the dish is bubbling hot and lightly brown on top. Let cool slightly before serving.

LAMB ROMANOFF
Serves 6

A fondness for spring lamb and the tang of dill and sour cream led us to create this delicate dish.

8 tablespoons oil
1 leg of lamb (4 pounds), cubed
5 tablespoons flour
2 cups beef consommé
2 tablespoons tomato paste
½ cup dry red wine
3 fresh dill sprigs or 1 tablespoon dried dill weed
Salt
Pepper
1½ pounds mushrooms, thinly sliced
6 tablespoons butter
Juice 1 large lemon
1 cup sour cream
2 tablespoons chopped fresh dill sprigs or 2 teaspoons
     dried dill weed

1. Heat 4 tablespoons of oil in a heavy skillet. Dry meat thoroughly, then sauté a few pieces at a time, browning on all sides. Remove meat and set aside.

2. Add remaining oil to pan and combine with the flour to make a smooth paste. Add the consommé gradually and the tomato paste and cook until thickened, stirring constantly. Stir in the red wine.

3. Return meat to skillet and add the dill and salt and

pepper to taste. Cover and cook 45 minutes over medium heat, or until meat is tender.

4. In a skillet, sauté the mushrooms briefly in the butter, then sprinkle with lemon juice and toss.

5. Add the mushrooms to the meat and cook together for 5 minutes. Remove from heat. Discard the sprigs of fresh dill.

6. Combine the sour cream with the chopped dill and stir into the meat.

A NOTE   Heat gently without boiling to prevent the sour cream from curdling, then serve on a bed of rice garnished with some fresh dill.

PORC BORDELAISE
Serves 6

While white meats are often prepared and served with white wine, this hearty dish, prepared with red wine, takes its inspiration from the traditional *coq au vin rouge*.

8 tablespoons butter
1 boneless pork roast (4 pounds), cut in 2-inch cubes
4 tablespoons flour
2 cups red Bordeaux wine
1 can (10½ ounces) bouillon
1 clove garlic, crushed
1 tablespoon tomato paste
1 teaspoon dried thyme
½ teaspoon dried marjoram
1 bay leaf

Salt
Pepper
¾ pound mushrooms, sliced
12 small white onions

1. Melt 2 tablespoons of butter in a heavy skillet and sauté the pork cubes until golden.

2. Remove the meat to a 4-quart casserole and, over low heat, toss the meat with the flour until all the pieces are thoroughly coated.

3. Deglaze the skillet by adding the Bordeaux wine and boiling rapidly while scraping the pan with a wooden spoon. Add this to the casserole with the undiluted bouillon.

4. Add the garlic, tomato paste, thyme, marjoram, bay leaf, and salt and pepper, combining well. Simmer covered about 2 hours until meat is tender.

5. While casserole is cooking, sauté the mushrooms in 3 tablespoons of butter until just wilted. Set contents of pan aside.

6. Sauté the onions in the remaining 3 tablespoons of butter until browned all over. Cover pan and cook until just tender.

7. Let the casserole cool slightly and remove excess fat. Stir in the mushrooms and onions and their juices.

A NOTE   Reheat thoroughly on the range and garnish with chopped parsley.

VEAL MARENGO
Serves 6 to 8

Marengo is a northern Italian village where Napoleon vanquished the Austrian troops. In honor of the victory Napoleon's chef created chicken Marengo, here adapted to veal.

4 tablespoons oil
4 pounds veal, cut in 2-inch cubes
4 tablespoons flour
2 medium onions, chopped
2 cloves garlic, chopped
1 cup dry white wine
1 cup beef stock
1½ cups well drained Italian-style tomatoes
½ teaspoon dried thyme
½ teaspoon dried tarragon
1 bay leaf
2 strips lemon peel
Salt
Pepper
2 tablespoons butter
½ pound mushrooms, sliced

1. In a heavy skillet, heat the oil and brown the veal cubes well on all sides, a few at a time.
2. Transfer the browned meat to a heavy 5-quart casserole and toss the veal with the flour until thoroughly coated.

3. In the skillet, sauté the onions and garlic until golden and add them to the casserole. Use additional oil if needed.

4. Pour the wine into the skillet, bringing it to a boil and scraping the bottom of the pan with a wooden spoon. Add the wine to the casserole, together with the stock, tomatoes, thyme, tarragon, bay leaf, lemon peel, and salt and pepper. Mix well, then cover and simmer gently about 2 hours, or until the meat is tender.

5. Remove the bay leaf and lemon peel from the casserole and skim off excess fat.

6. In a skillet, melt the butter and sauté the mushrooms, then add to the casserole.

A NOTE   Heat the casserole in a preheated 350 degree F. oven for 30 minutes, or until the meat is bubbling. Garnish with chopped parsley and serve with rice or noodles.

VITELLO TONNATO
Serves 6 to 8

A cold dish of Italian creation combining sliced veal, creamy tuna sauce, and tangy capers, and best made a day in advance.

1 boneless veal roast (4 pounds)
1 clove garlic, slivered
3 cups strong chicken stock
2 cups water
2 cups dry white wine
1 large onion, studded with 4 cloves

1 small bunch each celery leaves and parsley, tied
    together
Salt
Pepper
1 can (7 ounces) tuna fish, packed in oil
7 anchovy fillets
Juice 1 large lemon
1 egg yolk
½ cup oil
1 cup heavy cream

1. With a sharp knife, make small slits in the side of
the veal roast and insert the slivers of garlic.

2. Place the meat in a large heavy pot and cover it
with water. Bring to a boil and simmer 5 minutes, then
pour out the water.

3. Clean the scum from the pot and add to the veal the
stock, water, wine, onion, celery and parsley, salt, and
pepper. Let the veal simmer 1½ to 2 hours, or until
tender.

4. Remove the meat and let it cool completely. Then
chill for easy slicing.

5. In a blender place the tuna fish with its oil, anchovies, lemon juice, egg yolk, and oil, and process until
mixture is smooth and puréed. Stir in the cream.

6. Trim and slice the cooked veal. Cover with the
sauce and refrigerate.

A NOTE This is a splendid luncheon or supper dish, or
an unusual appetizer for an elegant dinner party. Lay
out the veal slices on a shallow platter and pour the sauce
over. Garnish with ¼ cup capers.

SHRIMP AEGEAN
Serves 6 to 8

Feta, a salty tangy white cheese from Greece, gives this shrimp dish its distinctive character.

6 tablespoons oil
2 onions, chopped
2 cloves garlic, chopped
1 (35 ounces) can Italian-style tomatoes
1 can (8 ounces) tomato sauce
¼ cup finely chopped parsley
1 tablespoon dried basil
1 teaspoon crushed fennel seeds
½ teaspoon sugar
Pepper
2 tablespoons butter
3 pounds raw shrimp, shelled and deveined
½ cup cognac
½ pound feta cheese, coarsely crumbled

1. In a heavy saucepan, heat 4 tablespoons of the oil and sauté the chopped onion and garlic until golden.
2. Add the tomatoes, tomato sauce, parsley, basil, crushed fennel seeds, sugar, and pepper and simmer uncovered until mixture begins to thicken.
3. In a large frying pan, heat the butter and remaining 2 tablespoons of oil and sauté the shrimp quickly until they just turn pink.
4. Warm the brandy and flame the shrimp.

5. Combine the shrimp in its brandied butter with tomato sauce in a pretty 3- or 4-quart ovenproof dish. Sprinkle the crumbled feta cheese on top.

A NOTE   Preheat the oven to 400 degrees F. and bake the dish for about 20 minutes or until the sauce is bubbling and the cheese is melted. Serve this Greek specialty on a bed of rice.

CHICKEN SALAD SUPREME
Serves 4 to 6

If you think there's nothing more to be done with chicken salad, try our favorite with the bite of chutney.

1 cup mayonnaise
½ cup sour cream
Juice 1 lemon
2 tablespoons chopped chutney
Salt
Pepper
4 cups cooked cubed chicken
1 pound seedless grapes
½ cup toasted slivered almonds

1. In a small bowl, combine the mayonnaise, sour cream, lemon juice, chutney, salt, and pepper for the dressing.
2. In a large bowl, combine the chicken, grapes, and almonds and toss with the dressing.

A NOTE   Mound the salad on a bed of lettuce leaves and garnish with hard-boiled egg halves.

TUNA SALAD NIÇOISE
Serves 6

Travelers to Mediterranean shores have long enjoyed this luncheon specialty, easily adapted to American kitchens.

½ cup oil
3 tablespoons Mixed Herb Vinegar
1 teaspoon dry mustard
Salt
Pepper
1 package (9 ounces) frozen artichoke hearts, cooked
    and cooled
1 package (9 ounces) frozen whole green beans, cooked
    crisp tender and cooled
1 small bunch scallions, coarsely chopped
2 cans (7 ounces each) tuna fish, drained and broken
    into chunks
⅔ cup halved pitted black olives
4 hard-boiled eggs, halved
4 tomatoes, cut in wedges

1. Combine the oil, vinegar, mustard, and salt and pepper for the dressing.

2. In a large mixing bowl, combine the artichokes, green beans, scallions, tuna fish, and olives and toss with the dressing.

3. Arrange the salad in the gift container and surround with egg halves and tomato wedges.

A NOTE   Serve salad on a bed of lettuce, if desired.

SPINACH SALAD WITH HAM AND MUSHROOMS
Serves 4

Fresh leafy spinach as a salad is rapidly gaining favor. Here it is combined with ham and raw mushrooms for a hot-weather lunch or supper.

6 tablespoons oil
2 tablespoons Mixed Herb Vinegar
1 teaspoon dry mustard
½ teaspoon finely chopped garlic
Salt
Pepper
½ pound cooked ham, cut in strips
½ pound mushrooms, wiped with damp cloth and
    thinly sliced
1 pound spinach, cleaned with stems removed
2 scallions, finely chopped

1. Mix the oil, vinegar, mustard, garlic, salt, and pepper together for the dressing. Store in covered jar.
2. In a large salad bowl, toss the ham, mushrooms, spinach, and scallions together.

A NOTE Toss salad with dressing and surround with hard-boiled egg halves and tomato wedges. Sprinkle with crumbled blue cheese if desired.

7

The Relish Tray

PRESERVES, RELISHES, pickles, and chutneys are the gourmet's summer and fall harvest. You can please a hostess at breakfast with exotic conserves and at dinner with enticing spiced fruits, pickled vegetables, and chutneys, sure to enhance even the most simply prepared chops and roasts.

All preserved food must be properly processed to prevent spoilage. The recipes in this chapter require a boiling water bath, which the U. S. Department of Agriculture recommends for all acid foods such as pickles, fruits, and tomatoes. (There are other processing methods for other kinds of foods.) You will need a water bath canner, which is a large pot deep enough so that 1 inch of water covers the tops of canning jars. It must have a rack to keep jars off the bottom of the pot and a cover to keep water at a rolling boil. You will also need to use canning jars which can withstand the heat of processing.

To process any of the recipes in this chapter, follow these steps:

1. Heat water in canner so it will be boiling when jars of food are ready to be processed.

2. Wash canning jars in hot soapy water. Work only with the number of jars that can be processed at one time in the canner.

3. Wash all foods thoroughly before cooking. Avoid overripe and blemished fruits and vegetables.

4. Prepare food according to recipes, then pack at once in clean jars to within ½ inch of the top.

5. Wipe rims of jars for tight seal, and cap according to jar manufacturer's directions.

6. Place filled jars in canner and begin counting processing time when water again comes to a boil.

7. When processing time is completed, remove jars immediately and set upright on cloth towels to cool.

To package these processed foods, look for containers that can accommodate half pint, pint, or quart jars. For instance:

Pack a sectional garden tote with the pickled bounty of the vegetable patch.

Line up an assortment of chutneys on a glass relish tray.

Assemble an appetizing variety of spiced fruits and pickled vegetables in a picnic hamper.

Collect a set of marmalades, jams, and conserves in a long French bread basket.

Wrap a large quart jar in a pretty kitchen towel or gay apron.

Or simply tie a colorful hair ribbon around the neck of a particularly favored delicacy and present in a bright and shiny paper tote bag.

APRICOT WALNUT CONSERVE
Makes five ½-pint jars

The combination of apricots, nuts, and citrus flavors makes this tart and crunchy conserve an excellent accompaniment to roast fowl and game.

1 pound dried apricots
1½ cups orange juice
Grated rind 1 medium orange
Juice 1 lemon
3½ cups sugar
¾ cup chopped walnuts

1. Cover apricots with water in a heavy stainless steel or enamel saucepan and simmer uncovered about 20 minutes, or until tender. Drain, then chop.
2. Return chopped apricots to saucepan and combine with orange juice, orange rind, lemon juice, and sugar. Bring to a boil and cook until mixture is thick, stirring constantly.
3. Remove from heat and stir in nuts.
4. Fill and cap containers according to manufacturer's instructions and process in hot water bath for 20 minutes.

PEACH PLUM JAM
Makes eight ½-pint jars

4 cups pitted, peeled, and diced peaches
4 cups pitted and diced red plums
7½ cups sugar
Grated rind and juice 1 lemon

1. In a large heavy stainless steel or enamel saucepan, combine all the ingredients. Cook, stirring constantly, until mixture comes to a boil and thickens.

2. Fill jars to within ½ inch of top. Cap containers according to manufacturer's instructions and process in hot water bath for 20 minutes.

PLUM NUT CONSERVE
Makes five ½-pint jars

This conserve makes a delicious alternative filling for our apricot pastry crescents.

2 pounds blue plums
¼ cup hot water
Grated rind and juice 1 orange
Grated rind and juice 1 lemon
1½ cups seedless raisins
3 cups sugar
1 cinnamon stick
1 cup broken walnuts

1. Wash and halve plums, removing stems and pits. Put in heavy stainless steel or enamel saucepan with the water.

2. Add the orange and lemon rinds and juice to the pot with the raisins, sugar, and cinnamon stick. Cook slowly until plums are transparent, about 20 minutes.

3. Add walnuts.

4. Fill jars to within ½ inch of the top. Cap containers according to manufacturer's instructions and process in hot water bath for 20 minutes.

SPICY BLUEBERRY PEACH PRESERVE
Makes eight ½-pint jars

Heat and serve this preserve as a sauce over bread pudding or unfrosted cakes.

4 cups blueberries, washed and stems removed
4 cups pitted, peeled, and diced peaches
Juice 1 lemon
½ cup water
5½ cups sugar
1 cinnamon stick ⎫
1 teaspoon whole allspice ⎭ tied in cheesecloth

1. In a heavy stainless steel or enamel saucepan combine the blueberries, peaches, lemon juice, and water and bring to a boil. Let simmer 15 minutes, stirring occasionally.
2. Add sugar and spices and let cook until mixture thickens.
3. Remove from heat and take out spices in cheesecloth.
4. Fill jars to within ½ inch of the top. Cap containers according to manufacturer's directions, and process in hot water bath for 20 minutes.

TOMATO LIME PRESERVE
Makes five ½-pint jars

We like to serve this unusual preserve with roast meat.

4 cups ripe peeled, chopped, and drained tomatoes
2 navel oranges, rind grated and pulp seeded and chopped
2 limes, rind grated and pulp seeded and chopped
3 cinnamon sticks
2 tablespoons chopped crystallized ginger
4 cups sugar

1. In a large heavy stainless steel or enamel saucepan, place all the ingredients and bring to a boil, stirring until the sugar is dissolved. Let the mixture simmer about 1 hour until thickened.
2. Remove from heat and take out cinnamon sticks.
3. Fill jars to within ½ inch of the top and cap containers according to manufacturer's directions. Process in a hot water bath for 20 minutes.

HONEY ORANGE SLICES
Makes three ½-pint jars

Here is a versatile treat: use the liquid to glaze a roast duck or roast pork, then garnish the platter with the orange slices.

4 large California oranges
1¼ cups sugar
1¼ cups honey
Juice 1 large lemon
3 cinnamon sticks
1½ teaspoons cloves
1½ teaspoons allspice

1. Slice oranges, discarding the end sections. Cut each slice in half.

2. Place the orange slices in a heavy stainless steel or enamel saucepan and cover with water. Bring to a boil and let simmer about 30 minutes, or until the rind is just tender. Drain well.

3. In the saucepan, combine the sugar, honey, and lemon juice and bring to a boil. Add the orange slices and cinnamon sticks and simmer for 40 minutes.

4. Put half a teaspoon of cloves and of allspice into each of the clean jars, then pack the orange slices and pour over the hot liquid to within ½ inch of the top. Cap containers according to manufacturer's instructions and process for 5 minutes in a hot water bath.

MIXED FRUIT MARMALADE
Makes eight ½-pint jars

4 oranges, thinly sliced and seeded
2 limes, thinly sliced and seeded
2 lemons, thinly sliced and seeded
Orange juice
Sugar

1. Measure the amount of sliced fruit in cups. Place fruit in a heavy enamel or stainless steel saucepan and add three times as many cups of orange juice as there are of fruit. Let stand overnight.

2. Bring contents of saucepan to a boil and let fruit and juice cook 20 minutes. Remove from heat and let stand overnight.

3. For every cup of the fruit-juice mixture, add ¾ cup of sugar. Bring mixture to a boil and cook 30 minutes, stirring occasionally to prevent scorching.

4. Remove from heat and skim off any foam.

5. Spoon contents into hot clean jars to within ½ inch of the top and cap according to manufacturer's directions. Process in a hot water bath for 15 minutes.

PEARS IN MADEIRA
Makes 2 pint jars

Wine-poached pears make a beautiful dessert by themselves or served with vanilla ice cream.

¾ cup sugar
½ cup Madeira wine
¼ cup water
1 quarter lemon
1 quarter large California orange
1 cinnamon stick
4 large pears, not quite ripe, peeled, halved, and cored

1. In a heavy stainless steel or enamel saucepan, combine the sugar, wine, water, lemon, orange, and cinnamon. Stir together and bring to a boil.

2. Poach the pear halves in the simmering liquid until just tender.

3. Remove the pears and place in clean pint jars.

4. Discard the lemon and orange quarters and simmer the syrup 5 minutes more. Pour over the pears in the jars to within ½ inch of the tops. Cap the jars according to the manufacturer's directions and process in a hot water bath for 20 minutes.

SPICED MELON RIND
Makes 6 pint jars

2 pounds watermelon rind, peeled and cubed
1 pound cantaloupe rind, peeled and cubed
¾ cup kosher salt
5 cups sugar
2 cups cider vinegar
1 cup water
1 tablespoon whole cloves ⎫
1 tablespoon whole allspice ⎭ tied in cheesecloth
4 cinnamon sticks
1 lemon, thinly sliced
6 teaspoons chopped candied lemon peel

1. Place the melon cubes in a large bowl and sprinkle with salt. Add water just to cover and let stand overnight.

2. Drain the melon cubes and place in a large saucepan. Cover with fresh cold water and bring to a boil. Let simmer until just tender and rind appears almost transparent.

3. Drain into colander.

4. In a large stainless steel or enamel saucepan, com-

bine sugar, vinegar, water, spices, cinnamon sticks, and lemon slices, and bring to a boil. Let simmer 5 minutes, then add the drained melon rind and continue cooking 10 to 15 minutes.

5. Remove from heat and discard spice bag, lemon slices, and cinnamon sticks.

6. Place 1 teaspoon of chopped candied lemon peel into each clean jar. Pack jars with the melon rind and pour syrup over to within ½ inch of the top. Cap according to manufacturer's directions and process in a hot water bath for 5 minutes.

SPICED PEACHES
Makes 7 quart jars

12 cups sugar
8 cups vinegar
7 cinnamon sticks
2 tablespoons whole cloves
1 tablespoon whole allspice
16 pounds medium-size peaches
Salt

1. In a large heavy stainless steel or enamel saucepan, combine the sugar, vinegar, cinnamon, cloves, and allspice and bring to a boil. Simmer 30 minutes.

2. Wash and peel peaches and immediately drop them into cold salted water to prevent discoloring.

3. Add a few peaches at a time to the boiling syrup, just enough to pack two jars at a time. Cook peaches for

5 minutes and remove them to clean quart jars with a slotted spoon.

4. When all the peaches have been cooked and packed, add one stick of cinnamon to each jar and pour in the boiling syrup to within ½ inch of the top of the jar. Cap according to the manufacturer's directions and process in a hot water bath for 20 minutes.

SPICED PINEAPPLE STICKS
Makes five ½-pint jars

Serve spiced pineapple sticks as a garnish for roast fowl, cut up in chicken salad, or in an après-ski punch bowl of hot mulled wine.

2 large pineapples
1 cup white vinegar
4 cups sugar
1 tablespoon cloves
1 tablespoon whole allspice
2 cinnamon sticks
1 large lemon, sliced

1. Remove ends of pineapple, and peel and core fruit. Cut into sticks 2½ inches long and ½ inch wide.

2. In a heavy stainless steel or enamel saucepan, combine the vinegar, sugar, cloves, allspice, cinnamon, and lemon slices. Bring to a boil, stirring constantly.

3. Add pineapple sticks and simmer 10 to 15 minutes, or until fruit becomes transparent.

4. Pack pineapple sticks vertically in clean jars.

5. Strain syrup and pour into jars to within ½ inch of the top. Cap jars according to manufacturer's directions and process 5 minutes in a hot water bath.

CHUTNEYS

CHUTNEYS MAY BE MADE all year round, using fresh fruit in season or dried fruits. Any of the following chutneys would be an excellent accompaniment to a curry dinner or add zest to other meat dishes.

APPLE CHUTNEY
Makes 3 pint jars

6 cups chopped and peeled apples
1 cup raisins
½ cup pitted chopped dates
1 cup minced onions
2 cloves garlic, minced
½ teaspoon crushed red pepper
Grated rind and juice 1 lemon
2 ounces preserved ginger, chopped
2 teaspoons salt
½ teaspoon cinnamon
½ teaspoon ground cloves
2¼ cups packed brown sugar
2 cups cider vinegar

1. Combine all the ingredients in a large stainless steel or enamel saucepan. Bring to a boil and simmer uncovered until thickened, about 3 hours. Stir occasionally.

2. Pour into clean jars to within ½ inch of the top. Cap according to manufacturer's directions and process in a hot water bath for 5 minutes.

BLUE PLUM CHUTNEY
Makes 4 pint jars

¾ cup cider vinegar
1 cup packed brown sugar
4 cups halved and pitted blue plums
¾ cup raisins
⅓ cup chopped onions
Grated rind and juice 1 lemon
⅓ cup finely chopped preserved ginger
3 cloves garlic, finely chopped
1 tablespoon mustard seed
½ teaspoon crushed red pepper
2 teaspoons salt
1 teaspoon allspice

1. In a heavy enamel or stainless steel saucepan bring vinegar to a boil and stir in the brown sugar.

2. Add the plums, raisins, onions, rind and juice of lemon, ginger, garlic, mustard seed, red pepper, salt, and allspice. Simmer about 1 hour, or until thickened.

3. Pour into clean jars to within ½ inch of the top and cap according to manufacturer's directions. Process in a hot water bath for 5 minutes.

CRANBERRY CHUTNEY
Makes 4 pint jars

4 cans (16 ounces each) whole cranberry sauce
1 cup pitted chopped dates
1 cup currants
1 cup slivered almonds
2 tablespoons chopped candied ginger
1 teaspoon allspice
1 cup packed brown sugar
1 cup cider vinegar

1. In a stainless steel or enamel saucepan, combine all the ingredients. Bring mixture to a boil, stirring constantly. Then simmer uncovered for 30 minutes or until thickened, stirring occasionally.
2. Pack chutney in clean jars to within ½ inch of the top and cap according to manufacturer's directions. Process in a hot water bath for 5 minutes.

DRIED FRUIT CHUTNEY
Makes 6 pint jars

1½ cups coarsely chopped dried apricots
1½ cups coarsely chopped dried peaches
1 cup currants
4 cups cider vinegar
1 cup granulated sugar

2 cups packed brown sugar
Grated rind and juice 1 lemon
1 cup chopped onions
½ cup chopped preserved ginger
3 cloves garlic, finely chopped
1 teaspoon crushed red pepper
1 tablespoon salt
1 teaspoon cinnamon
1 teaspoon allspice
1 teaspoon coriander

1. In a large enamel or stainless steel saucepan, soak the apricots, peaches, and currants in the vinegar about 1 hour to soften.

2. Stir in the granulated and brown sugar. Add the lemon rind and juice, onions, ginger, garlic, red pepper, salt, cinnamon, allspice, and coriander, and mix well.

3. Cook mixture about 1 hour or until thick.

4. Pack chutney into clean jars to within ½ inch of the top and cap according to manufacturer's directions. Process in a hot water bath for 15 minutes.

PICKLED VEGETABLES

IN A DELECTABLE VARIETY of colors, tastes, and shapes, pickled vegetables are favorites on the relish tray and a pleasure to have on hand, all of which makes a selection of them eminently giftworthy.

BASIL GREEN BEANS
Makes 7 pint jars

4 pounds green string beans
1¾ teaspoons crushed red pepper
3½ teaspoons whole mustard seed
3½ teaspoons dill seed
14 cloves garlic, peeled
1 bunch fresh basil or 3½ teaspoons dried basil
5 cups Basil Vinegar
5 cups water
½ cup salt

1. Wash, then cut whole string beans evenly to fit the height of a pint jar. Pack beans vertically in clean jars and add to each jar ¼ teaspoon crushed red pepper, ½ teaspoon whole mustard seed, ½ teaspoon dill seed, 2 cloves garlic, and a sprig of fresh basil or ½ teaspoon dried basil.

2. In a large stainless steel or enamel saucepan, combine the vinegar, water, and salt, and bring to a boil.

3. Pour the boiling liquid over the beans in each jar to within ½ inch of the top. Cap according to manufacturer's directions and process in a hot water bath for 10 minutes.

PICKLED BEETS
Makes 4 pint jars

4 pounds small beets, cooked and skinned
2 cups liquid in which beets were cooked
2 cups cider vinegar
2 cups sugar
2 tablespoons dry mustard
1 tablespoon allspice
1 tablespoon cinnamon
1 teaspoon peppercorns
2 bay leaves

1. Combine all the ingredients in a large stainless steel or enamel saucepan. Bring to a boil and cook for 5 minutes.
2. Pack beets in clean jars, and fill with boiling liquid to within ½ inch of the top. Cap according to manufacturer's directions and process in a hot water bath for 25 minutes.

PICKLED CARROT STICKS
Makes seven ½-pint jars

2 pounds carrots
1¾ teaspoons crushed red pepper
1¾ teaspoons whole mustard seed
1¾ teaspoons dill seed

7 cloves garlic
1 bunch fresh mint or 3½ teaspoons dried mint leaves
2½ cups Mint Vinegar
2½ cups water
3 tablespoons sugar
3 tablespoons salt

1. Scrape carrots, then cut into thin sticks. Cut evenly to fit the height of the ½-pint jars.
2. Pack carrots vertically in jars, then add to each jar ¼ teaspoon crushed red pepper, ¼ teaspoon mustard seed, ¼ teaspoon dill seed, 1 clove garlic, and a large sprig of fresh mint or ½ teaspoon dried mint leaves.
3. In a large stainless steel or enamel saucepan, combine the vinegar, water, sugar, and salt. Bring to a boil.
4. Pour boiling liquid into each jar to within ½ inch of the top. Cap according to manufacturer's directions and process in hot water bath for 10 minutes.

PICKLED CAULIFLOWER FLORETS
Makes 5 pint jars

8 cups cauliflower florets
1 cup chopped red pepper
1 cup chopped green pepper
2 cups chopped onions
3½ cups white vinegar
1½ cups sugar
1 tablespoon mustard seed
1 tablespoon celery seed
1 teaspoon cloves
¼ teaspoon dried red pepper

1. Blanch cauliflower florets in boiling water for 2 minutes. Drain.

2. In a large stainless steel or enamel saucepan, combine the red and green peppers, onion, vinegar, sugar, mustard seed, celery seed, cloves, and dried red pepper. Bring to a boil and simmer 5 minutes, stirring occasionally.

3. Add the cauliflower and continue simmering for 10 minutes, or until the cauliflower is tender but still crisp.

4. Pack the florets into clean jars and pour boiling liquid to within ½ inch of the top. Cap according to manufacturer's directions. Process in a hot water bath for 5 minutes.

VEGETABLE RELISHES

VEGETABLE RELISHES enhance beef dishes from hamburger to prime rib roast. Take advantage of the autumn abundance of these vegetables in your garden and at roadside stands.

GREEN TOMATO RELISH
Makes 4 pint jars

5 cups chopped green tomatoes
5 cups chopped cabbage
2 large green peppers, chopped
2 large red peppers, chopped
3 large onions, chopped
1/3 cup salt
3 cups cider vinegar
1 cup granulated sugar
1 cup packed brown sugar
2 tablespoons whole mixed pickling spice, tied in cheese-
    cloth

1. In a large bowl, combine the tomatoes, cabbage, green and red peppers, and onions with the salt. Let stand overnight.
2. Drain vegetables and press out excess liquid.
3. In a large stainless steel or enamel saucepan, combine vinegar, granulated and brown sugar, and spice bag and bring to a boil. Add the drained vegetables and bring to another boil. Simmer 30 minutes, or until most of the liquid has evaporated and the relish has thickened to desired consistency. Remove spice bag.
4. Pack in clean jars to within 1/2 inch of the top and cap according to manufacturer's directions. Process in boiling water bath for 5 minutes.

PICCADILLY PICCALILLI
Makes 4 pint jars

6 small cucumbers, sliced
3 cups cauliflower florets
2 cups tiny white onions
2 green peppers, chopped
2 red peppers, chopped
½ cup salt
3 cups cider vinegar
1 teaspoon celery seed
1 teaspoon cloves
1 teaspoon allspice
1 teaspoon turmeric
¼ cup dry mustard
¼ cup flour

1. In a large mixing bowl, place layers of cucumber slices, cauliflower florets, onions, green and red peppers, sprinkling the salt between each layer. Let stand overnight.

2. Drain to remove excess liquid.

3. In a large heavy stainless steel or enamel saucepan, heat the vinegar with the celery seed, cloves, and allspice to boiling and add the drained vegetables. Simmer 20 minutes, or until tender.

4. Mix the turmeric, dry mustard, and flour with enough cold water to make a smooth paste and add to the saucepan. Continue simmering 10 more minutes.

5. Pack piccalilli in clean jars to within ½ inch of the top and cap according to manufacturer's directions. Process in a hot water bath for 5 minutes.

SWEET MIXED PEPPER RELISH
Makes 4 pint jars

4 green peppers, finely chopped
4 red peppers, finely chopped
4 onions, finely chopped
1 cup cider vinegar
1 cup sugar
1 tablespoon salt
1 teaspoon garlic salt

1. Combine all the ingredients in a large stainless steel or enamel saucepan. Bring to a boil and simmer 10 minutes.

2. Drain relish and reserve liquid.

3. Spoon relish loosely into clean jars, then pour reserved liquid into jars to within ½ inch of the top. Cap according to manufacturer's directions and process in a boiling water bath for 5 minutes.

ZUCCHINI RELISH
Makes 4 pint jars

4 cups finely chopped zucchini
2 cups finely chopped onions
2 cups finely chopped green tomatoes
1 cup finely chopped green pepper
1 cup finely chopped red pepper

4 tablespoons salt
1 cup sugar
2 cups cider vinegar
1 tablespoon dry mustard
1 teaspoon turmeric
2 teaspoons celery seed

1. In a large bowl, combine the zucchini, onions, green tomatoes, green and red peppers, and salt. Let stand overnight.

2. Drain vegetables and press out excess liquid.

3. In a large stainless steel or enamel saucepan, combine the sugar, vinegar, mustard, turmeric, and celery seed. Bring to a boil.

4. Add drained vegetables and bring to a boil. Simmer uncovered about 40 minutes, or until relish has thickened to desired consistency.

5. Pack in clean jars to within ½ inch of top and cap according to manufacturer's directions. Process in hot water bath for 10 minutes.

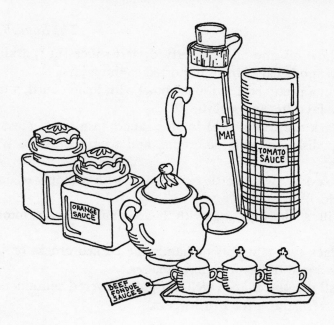

8

The Sauceboat

SAUCES, DRESSINGS, and marinades are the surest way to confer gourmet status on a friend, for nothing so dresses up a dish as a delectable sauce. The recipes in this chapter are planned to enhance entire meals, from appetizers through desserts.

Packaging sauces naturally requires covered containers. For example:

Pack hard sauces in a pair of brandy snifters.

Show off any of the pretty dessert sauces in sparkling glass apothecary jars or imported canning jars.

Fill a pretty covered sugar bowl with lemon curd, a teatime favorite, and seal the lid.

Pack the trio of beef fondue sauces in a set of covered soup dishes or pots de crème, and secure the tops with tape.

Recycle a wine bottle or decanter with a supply of marinade.

Fill a thermos jug with hearty barbecue or tomato sauce.

Pack two jam pots or handsome corked crocks or jars with a pair of flavored mayonnaises.

All the sauces keep well in tightly covered containers in the refrigerator for 1 to 3 weeks.

SUNDAE SAUCES

You CAN'T BUY old-time sundae fixings any more, so we fill the gap with these extra-rich and gooey fudge and butterscotch sauces.

ALL-AMERICAN FUDGE SAUCE
Makes 2 cups

½ cup butter
4 ounces semi-sweet chocolate
½ cup cocoa
½ cup sugar
1 cup light cream
1 teaspoon vanilla

1. In a heavy saucepan, melt the butter and chocolate together.
2. Mix the cocoa with ¼ cup of the sugar and stir in. Add the cream, then the remaining ¼ cup of sugar. Bring mixture to a boil, stirring constantly to prevent scorching.
3. Remove from heat immediately and add vanilla. Cool, then refrigerate.

A NOTE   To reheat fudge sauce, place container in pan of hot water until sauce reaches pouring consistency.

BUTTERSCOTCH SAUCE
Makes 2 cups

1½ cups packed brown sugar
¾ cup corn syrup
¾ cup heavy cream
¼ cup butter
⅛ teaspoon salt
2 teaspoons vanilla

1. In a heavy saucepan, combine the sugar, corn syrup, cream, butter, and salt. Bring to a boil and stir constantly until sugar is dissolved.
2. Insert a candy thermometer and continue cooking until temperature reaches 238 degrees F.
3. Remove from heat and stir in vanilla.

A NOTE   A traditional favorite over ice cream, but try it also on angel cake or hot pudding.

CHOCOLATE FONDUES

THIS DESSERT SAUCE for dunking was originally created in Switzerland to promote their famous chocolate, a happy circumstance for chocolate lovers the world over.

CHOCOLATE FONDUE GRAND MARNIER
Serves 6

8 ounces sweet baking chocolate
⅔ cup light cream
2 tablespoons Grand Marnier

1. In the top of a double boiler over hot (but not boiling) water, melt the chocolate in the cream.
2. When the mixture is smooth, remove from the heat and stir in the Grand Marnier.
3. Refrigerate in a covered container.

A NOTE   Warm this elegant dessert sauce over hot water and maintain the temperature over a candle flame (any stronger heat may scorch the chocolate). Serve it with long forks and a variety of tidbits for spearing and dipping: grapes, strawberries, pineapple chunks, orange and pear slices, miniature cream puff shells, nut cake squares, macaroons, spongecake bits. If a suitable occasion for such festivities is not immediately at hand, you may keep the fondue for weeks in a covered container in the refrigerator.

MILK CHOCOLATE FONDUE
Serves 6

8 ounces sweet baking chocolate
1 cup heavy cream
2 tablespoons superfine sugar
1 teaspoon vanilla

1. In the top of a double boiler over hot (but not boiling) water, melt the chocolate in the cream.
2. When the mixture is smooth, stir in the sugar and vanilla.
3. Refrigerate in a covered container.

A NOTE   This is the youth version of chocolate fondue, guaranteed to enliven any party. Warm the fondue over hot water and maintain the temperature over a candle flame (any stronger heat may scorch the chocolate). Serve a smörgåsbord of goodies for dunking: toasted angel food cake, ladyfingers, brownie bites, marshmallows, maraschino cherries, nougats, popcorn, banana and apple slices.

ENGLISH LEMON CURD
Makes 3 cups

Virtually every English home has lemon curd on hand to serve with toasted scones or biscuits at high tea. Americans have found many other delicious uses for this tangy treat.

5 eggs
2 cups sugar
10 tablespoons butter, melted
Grated rind and juice 3 lemons

1. Beat eggs well. Add sugar gradually, beating continuously. Add the melted butter, rind and juice of lemons, and combine well.
2. Cook mixture in a double boiler, stirring constantly, until thick.
3. Cool and store in covered jar in refrigerator.

A NOTE   Use lemon curd as a tart filling between layers of sponge or angel cake or in a lemon meringue pie.

FRUIT SAUCES

THE MARRIAGE of fresh fruit and liqueur is an extravagant perfection to delight any hostess. Herewith is a trio of superb fruit sauces.

FRESH PEACH SAUCE
Makes 4 cups

16 peaches (about 4 pounds), peeled, sliced, and pitted
Juice 3 lemons
1 tablespoon grated lemon rind
2 cups sugar
1 cinnamon stick
3 tablespoons Cointreau or Grand Marnier

1. In a heavy saucepan, heat the peach slices and lemon juice slowly, stirring constantly until mixture comes to a boil.
2. Add the lemon rind, sugar, and cinnamon stick and continue cooking for 10 minutes, stirring occasionally to prevent scorching.
3. Remove sauce from heat and stir in the liqueur.

A NOTE   Perfection over ice cream or cake. Garnish with slivered almonds if desired.

FRESH PINEAPPLE IN KIRSCH
Makes 3 to 4 cups

1 large pineapple, peeled and cored
2 to 3 cups sugar
2 tablespoons chopped candied ginger
½ cup kirsch

1. Cut pineapple into thick slices and then into bite-size chunks and remove all brown sections. Measure the cut fruit by cups.
2. Place the fruit with an equal amount of sugar in a large ceramic crock or glass jar. Add the ginger and kirsch. Stir the ingredients together carefully. Cover and store in a cool place.
3. Stir pineapple mixture every day for 1 week. Then over an additional 3 or 4 weeks stir occasionally while fruit marinates. Always cover and store in cool place.
4. Pack pineapple sauce in jars and store in refrigerator.

A NOTE   Absolutely elegant over ice cream.

STRAWBERRY SAUCE
Makes 2 cups

2 cups hulled and sliced fresh strawberries
2 tablespoons superfine sugar or Orange Sugar
2 tablespoons cognac

1. Process the fruit, sugar, and cognac in the blender until mixture is puréed.

2. Refrigerate sauce several hours for perfect blending of flavors.

A NOTE Superb on ice cream, cold lemon or orange soufflés, or on spongecake.

HARD SAUCES

HARD SAUCES are traditionally associated with the Christmas season, but their virtues extend all year long.

BRANDIED HARD SAUCE
Makes 1 cup

6 tablespoons butter
1½ cups sifted confectioners' sugar
1 teaspoon vanilla
2 tablespoons brandy
Pinch salt

   1. Cream the butter thoroughly, then beat in the sugar slowly until well blended and fluffy.
   2. Add the vanilla, brandy, and salt and mix well.
   3. Chill in its gift container.

A NOTE   Pressed in individual butter molds, hard sauce is attractively served on Christmas plum puddings and on warm spicy gingerbread.

SOUTHERN HARD SAUCE
Makes 1¼ cups

6 tablespoons butter
1¼ cups firmly packed light brown sugar
¼ cup heavy cream
1 teaspoon vanilla
¼ cup chopped pecans
Pinch salt

1. Cream the butter thoroughly, then beat in the sugar slowly until well blended.

2. Add the cream, vanilla, nuts, and salt and mix well.

3. Chill in its gift container.

A NOTE   Try this on baked puddings, hot mince pie, or waffles.

SAUCES FOR MEAT

SIMPLY PREPARED meat and poultry dishes become dinner-party fare with the addition of an appropriate sauce. Here is a group of such sauces to enhance a variety of meat dishes.

BING CHERRY SAUCE
Makes 2 cups

1 jar (16 ounces) bing cherries
Juice 1 large orange
Juice 1 lemon
1 teaspoon dry mustard
1 teaspoon ginger
½ cup packed brown sugar
¼ cup granulated sugar
1 tablespoon cornstarch
4 tablespoons kirsch
⅓ cup slivered almonds
1 tablespoon grated orange peel

1. Drain cherries and reserve juice.
2. In a saucepan, combine the cherry juice with the orange and lemon juice, mustard, ginger, brown and granulated sugar, and cornstarch. Mix thoroughly. Bring to a boil over medium heat and simmer sauce for 15 minutes.
3. Add the cherries and continue cooking 15 minutes more, stirring occasionally, until the sauce thickens.
4. Remove sauce from heat and stir in the kirsch, almonds, and orange peel.

A NOTE   Heat sauce gently and serve with duck, chicken, and rock Cornish hen.

CHINESE PLUM SAUCE
Makes 1½ cups

1 cup plum preserves
½ cup chutney
1 tablespoon sugar
1 tablespoon vinegar

Put all the ingredients in a blender and process at high speed.

A NOTE   In its traditional role, this sauce is served with Chinese meat dishes. It's also a lovely glaze or accompaniment for ham, pork, spareribs, and duck.

CUMBERLAND SAUCE
Makes 2 cups

1 orange
1 lemon
½ cup currant jelly
1 cup port wine
½ teaspoon ginger
1 teaspoon dry mustard
1 teaspoon cornstarch
½ cup currants
½ cup slivered almonds

1. Extract the juice of the orange and lemon, strain and set aside.

2. Cut the skin of half the orange and half the lemon into julienne strips, removing the white part. Place strips in a small saucepan, cover with cold water, bring to a boil, and simmer 10 minutes. Drain and set aside.

3. In a saucepan, melt the currant jelly over low heat, and stir in the wine, orange and lemon juices.

4. Combine the ginger, mustard, and cornstarch with enough water to make a smooth paste, and add to the saucepan, stirring well. Bring mixture to a boil and let simmer until slightly thickened.

5. Add drained rind, currants, and almonds and simmer 2 more minutes.

A NOTE This is traditionally served with ham, tongue, or game.

PIQUANT MADEIRA SAUCE
Makes 2 cups

1½ tablespoons butter
1½ tablespoons flour
1 cup apple cider
¼ cup brown sugar
2 tablespoons lemon juice
1 teaspoon grated lemon rind
½ cup raisins
½ cup Madeira wine

1. In a heavy saucepan, melt the butter. Remove from heat and stir in flour to form a smooth paste. Return to heat and cook 1 minute, stirring constantly. Gradually

add apple cider and continue cooking until sauce is
slightly thickened.

2. Stir in sugar, lemon juice, lemon rind, raisins, and
wine and let stand on very low heat until raisins are
plump and flavors are well combined.

A NOTE   Serve with ham and other smoked meat.

SAUCE BORDELAISE
Makes 2 cups

¼ cup finely chopped shallots or scallions (white part
      only)
4 tablespoons butter
1 cup dry red wine
1 bay leaf
5 peppercorns
1 clove garlic, unpeeled
½ pound mushrooms, sliced
1 cup canned brown sauce
1 teaspoon lemon juice
1 tablespoon finely chopped fresh parsley leaves

1. Sauté the shallots or scallions in 2 tablespoons of
the butter until golden.

2. Add the wine, bay leaf, peppercorns, and garlic, and
reduce mixture to one half its original volume.

3. While the mixture is reducing, sauté the mushrooms
in the remaining 2 tablespoons of butter and set aside.

4. Press the reduced mixture through a sieve and stir

in the brown sauce, lemon juice, parsley, and sautéed mushrooms.

A NOTE Heat gently in the top of a double boiler and serve with chops, steaks, and roast meat.

TOMATO SAUCE
Makes 1 quart

4 tablespoons oil
2 onions, chopped
3 cloves garlic, chopped
1 large can (28 ounces) Italian-style tomatoes
1 large can (12 ounces) tomato paste
1 can (10½ ounces) beef bouillon
1 can (10½ ounces) water
2 teaspoons dried basil
2 teaspoons oregano
½ teaspoon crushed anise seeds
Salt
Pepper

1. In a large heavy saucepan, heat the oil and sauté the onions and garlic until golden.
2. Add tomatoes, tomato paste, bouillon, and water. Stir well and simmer uncovered for 2 hours.
3. Add basil, oregano, crushed anise seeds, salt, and pepper, and continue cooking over low heat for another ½ hour, or until sauce has thickened to desired consistency.

A NOTE Use with pasta and meat loaf, and try with shrimp and fish dishes. Keeps about 1 week in the refrigerator.

VINAIGRETTE SAUCE
Makes 1 cup

¾ cup olive oil
¼ cup Mixed Herb Vinegar
2 tablespoons minced shallots
1 teaspoon dry mustard
2 teaspoons capers
1 teaspoon salt
¼ teaspoon pepper

Combine all the ingredients and store in a tightly capped jar in refrigerator.

A NOTE This vinaigrette sauce has an excellent way with cold meat, fish, and vegetable dishes.

BEEF FONDUE SAUCES

A SOPHISTICATED do-it-yourself dinner party might likely feature beef fondue, the table-top cookery in which guests cook raw beef cubes in a communal pot of sizzling oil. Here is a trio of sauces to serve with beef fondue.

HORSERADISH SAUCE
Makes 1¼ cups

1 cup sour cream
¼ cup well-drained prepared horseradish
1 teaspoon salt
2 tablespoons snipped fresh chives
½ teaspoon grated lemon rind

Combine all the ingredients in a bowl and let stand in refrigerator at least 1 hour.

A NOTE   Serve as an accompaniment to beef fondue.

MUSTARD SAUCE
Makes 1¼ cups

1 egg
½ teaspoon salt
½ clove garlic
2 tablespoons lemon juice
2 tablespoons Dijon mustard
1 cup oil

1. Break the egg into a blender container, and add the salt, garlic, lemon juice, mustard, and 2 tablespoons of the oil. Cover and process at low speed until blended.

2. Uncover container and, while blender is still operating, slowly add the remaining oil in a thin steady stream.

A NOTE   Serve as an accompaniment to beef fondue.

TOMATO CURRY
Makes 1 cup

3 tablespoons oil
1 clove garlic, pressed
1 tablespoon curry powder
1 can (17 ounces) Italian-style tomatoes, drained
Salt
Pepper

1. In a saucepan, heat the oil and sauté the garlic and curry powder until golden.

2. Add the tomatoes, salt, and pepper and cook uncovered 30 minutes, or until most of the water has evaporated.

A NOTE   Serve as an accompaniment to beef fondue.

BARBECUE SAUCES

HERE ARE TWO BARBECUE SAUCES of widely different taste, at home on the range indoors and out.

CHILI BARBECUE SAUCE
Makes 1¼ cups

1 cup canned tomato sauce
2 tablespoons soy sauce
2 tablespoons A-1 sauce
2 cloves garlic, pressed
Juice 1 large lemon
2 tablespoons chili powder
2 tablespoons brown sugar

Combine all the ingredients in a saucepan and simmer 10 minutes.

A NOTE   Use for basting spareribs, pork, or beef.

ISLAND BARBECUE SAUCE
Makes 1¼ cups

½ cup orange marmalade
½ cup medium dry sherry
4 tablespoons soy sauce
2 large cloves garlic, mashed
1 teaspoon ginger
1 teaspoon coriander

Combine all the ingredients in a saucepan and simmer 5 minutes, stirring occasionally.

A NOTE   Use for basting chicken, duck, veal, or pork.

MOCK HOLLANDAISE
Makes 1¼ cups

This light and tangy sauce is easy to make, keeps beautifully, and has myriad uses.

2 egg yolks
Juice 1 lemon
4 tablespoons water
⅛ teaspoon salt
½ pint sour cream

1. In the top of a double boiler, combine with a whisk the egg yolks, lemon juice, water, and salt. Heat until the mixture thickens.
2. Remove from heat and let cool slightly.
3. Stir in the sour cream. Refrigerate.

A NOTE   A splendid sauce for asparagus and broccoli, tuna and salmon, hot or cold. If sauce is served warm, heat over hot, not boiling water.

FLAVORED MAYONNAISES

HOMEMADE MAYONNAISE is infinitely better than its store-bought counterpart, and simple to prepare in a blender. We offer two flavored mayonnaises to enhance meat, fish, and vegetable dishes.

CURRY MAYONNAISE
Makes 1¼ cups

1 egg
½ teaspoon salt
1 teaspoon dry mustard
½ clove garlic
1 teaspoon curry powder
2 tablespoons lemon juice
1 cup oil
2 tablespoons heavy cream

1. Break the egg into blender container, and add the salt, mustard, garlic, curry powder, lemon juice, and 2 tablespoons of the oil. Cover and process at low speed until blended.
2. Uncover container and, while blender is still operating, slowly pour in remaining oil in a thin steady stream.
3. Stir in heavy cream.

A NOTE Serve with cold chicken, fish, or vegetable salad.

DILL MAYONNAISE
Makes 1¼ cups

1 egg
½ teaspoon salt
1 teaspoon dry mustard
2 tablespoons cider vinegar
1 tablespoon chopped fresh dill sprigs
1 tablespoon chopped fresh chives
1 cup oil

1. Break the egg into blender container, and add the salt, mustard, vinegar, dill, chives, and 2 tablespoons of the oil. Cover and process at low speed until blended.

2. Uncover container and, while blender is still operating, slowly pour in the remaining oil in a thin steady stream.

A NOTE   Serve with shrimp, lobster, or crab meat salad.

REMOULADE SAUCE
Makes 1½ cups

1 egg
1 teaspoon Dijon mustard
1 tablespoon Mixed Herb Vinegar
1 cup oil
½ teaspoon salt

1 tablespoon capers
1 teaspoon dried tarragon
Juice ½ lemon
1 tablespoon chopped fresh parsley leaves
3 scallions, finely chopped

1. Process in a blender the egg, mustard, vinegar, ¼ cup of the oil, and salt.

2. While blender is running, add the remaining ¾ cup oil in a steady slow stream and blend until the mixture is thick and creamy.

3. Remove jar from blender and stir in the capers, tarragon, lemon juice, parsley, and scallions. Combine well and chill.

A NOTE   Serve remoulade sauce over cold shellfish.

MARINADES

MARINADES ARE a pleasure to have on hand; they keep well, improve with age, and in a few hours they can transform a simple meat dish into a culinary delight. Here is a trio of marinades that make splendid gifts.

CURRY MARINADE
Makes 1 cup

½ cup lemon juice
½ cup oil
½ medium onion, grated
2 cloves garlic, mashed
1 teaspoon coriander
½ teaspoon ginger
1 tablespoon curry powder
1 teaspoon salt

Combine all the ingredients in a screw-top jar and shake well. Store in refrigerator.

A NOTE   Wonderful for marinating skewered lamb. Keep refrigerated.

HAWAIIAN MARINADE
Makes about 1½ cups

¼ cup salad oil
¼ cup lime juice
¼ cup pineapple juice

¼ cup soy sauce
½ cup rum
1 large clove garlic, pressed
2 tablespoons light molasses
1 tablespoon ginger
1 teaspoon dry mustard

Combine all ingredients in a tightly capped jar and shake well. Store in refrigerator.

A NOTE This is an excellent marinade for pork and chicken dishes. Keep in refrigerator.

SAVORY MARINADE
Makes 1 cup

½ cup oil
¼ cup lemon juice
¼ cup dry red wine
2 tablespoons Worcestershire sauce
2 cloves garlic, mashed
2 teaspoons paprika
1 teaspoon salt
Pepper

Combine all the ingredients in a screw-top jar and shake well. Store in refrigerator.

A NOTE An excellent way to enhance the flavor of grilled beef. Keep refrigerated.

9

The Cookie Crock

KEEPING THE COOKIE JAR FILLED often seems like a never-ending task, so it's no wonder that cookies are always welcome gifts. Here is an assortment of bars, drop cookies, nut cookies, refrigerator cookies, and rolled cookies to meet the exacting standards of young and old alike.

All the cookies and bars in this chapter keep best in an airtight container, and all freeze well. As for packaging, your main concern will be to protect cookies from breaking and bars from sticking. Use cellophane or plastic wrap liberally, crumpled and in sheets to separate or layer the cookies. As for containers, here are some ideas that come to mind:

Pack a "Tea" canister with chocolate-glazed tea cookies and a matching "Coffee" canister with cinnamon apple-sauce squares.

Carefully pack pecan snowballs or almond crescents into a humidor.

Mound chocolate almond crisps or apricot pastry crescents in an elegant Lucite wine cooler.

Fill a cachepot with madeleines or bear paws.

Heap koulourakia or butter-nut crisps in a crystal pitcher.

Stow old-fashioned sugar rounds, date nut bars, chocolate meringue puffs, or the bridge assortment in plastic bags and nestle them in a mesh salad basket.

To delight a child, pack brownies or hermits or coconut oatmeal crisps in a sand pail, pile a toy wheelbarrow high with peanut butter cookies or molasses snaps, hide golden coconut drops in a bird feeder.

ALMOND CRESCENTS
Makes 60 cookies

A classic, melt-in-the-mouth Viennese specialty.

1 cup butter, softened
½ cup granulated sugar
2 teaspoons vanilla
2 cups flour
1¼ cups ground almonds
Confectioners' sugar

1. Cream the butter. Gradually add the granulated sugar and beat until light and fluffy. Add the vanilla.
2. Stir in the flour and nuts and mix until well blended. Form dough into a smooth ball, wrap in wax paper, and refrigerate for 1 hour for easy handling.
3. Preheat oven to 350 degrees F.
4. Working with 1 teaspoon of dough at a time, form tapered cylinders about 2 to 3 inches long. Shape these into crescents and place on ungreased baking sheets 1 inch apart.
5. Bake about 15 minutes, or until light golden.
6. When crescents are slightly cooled, sift on a light dusting of confectioners' sugar.

APRICOT PASTRY CRESCENTS
Makes 64 cookies

These are made from standard cream cheese pastry dough rolled around an apricot-nut filling.

½ pound cream cheese, softened
½ pound butter, softened
2 cups flour
½ teaspoon salt
⅓ cup cold water
1 teaspoon vanilla
½ cup chopped walnuts
¾ cup golden raisins
½ cup apricot jam
¼ cup cinnamon sugar

1. In a large bowl, cut the cream cheese and butter into the flour and salt with a pastry blender until thoroughly blended.

2. Mix water and vanilla and sprinkle over dough. Mix together well.

3. Refrigerate dough overnight.

4. Preheat oven to 425 degrees F.

5. Combine the chopped walnuts, raisins, and apricot jam.

6. Divide dough into quarters and, keeping dough refrigerated until ready to use, work with one quarter at a time. Form each quarter of the dough into a ball and roll out on a floured board into a 12-inch circle. Sprinkle each circle with 1 tablespoon of cinnamon sugar. Cut circles of dough in half, then in quarters, and finally into 16 wedges.

7. Place ½ teaspoon of the fruit and nut filling at the wide end of each wedge and roll up tightly toward the point. Place the rolled crescents point down on ungreased cookie sheets and bake 15 to 20 minutes, or until golden.

8. Cool slightly, then store in a tightly capped container.

A NOTE For fresh-from-the-oven taste, warm crescents in a 300 degree F. oven for 15 minutes.

BEAR PAWS
Makes 48 cookies

A rich, crisp nut cookie baked in madeleine pans to form the decorative shape from which this unusual cookie gets its name.

1 cup butter, softened
¾ cup granulated sugar
2½ cups flour
1 can (4 ounces) unblanched almonds, ground
1 teaspoon cinnamon
¼ teaspoon ground cloves
Superfine sugar

1. Cream the butter, then beat in the sugar. Add the flour, almonds, cinnamon, and cloves and mix well.
2. Chill the dough for at least 1 hour.
3. Preheat the oven to 350 degrees F. and butter madeleine pans carefully and well.
4. Press about 2 tablespoons of dough into each madeleine form.
5. Bake for 15 to 20 minutes, or until brown.
6. Turn cookies out onto a board sprinkled with superfine sugar and dust the tops of the cookies lightly with additional sugar. Cool.

BEST BROWNIES
Makes forty-eight 1½-inch squares

A moist and fudgy version of a favorite treat.

4 ounces baking chocolate
1 cup butter, softened
2 cups sugar
4 eggs
1 cup flour
1 cup chopped nuts
2 teaspoons vanilla

1. Preheat oven to 350 degrees F. and butter a 9×13-inch pan.
2. Melt the chocolate over hot, not boiling, water and set aside to cool.
3. Cream the butter well, then add the sugar slowly and continue to beat until the mixture is light and fluffy.
4. Beat in the eggs one at a time.
5. Mix in the melted chocolate.
6. Add the flour, and beat until it is incorporated in the batter. Stir in the nuts and vanilla.
7. Pour the batter into the prepared pan and bake for 35 minutes.
8. Cool before cutting into squares.

BRIDGE ASSORTMENT
Makes about 5 dozen

Heart, spade, club, and diamond shapes make this cookie fun to share with friends. You can also cut out other favorite shapes from the rolled dough.

3 cups sifted flour
1 teaspoon salt
½ teaspoon baking powder
½ cup butter, softened
½ cup shortening
¾ cup sugar
1 egg
1 teaspoon vanilla
Grated rind 1 lemon

1. Sift the flour, salt, and baking powder together and set aside.
2. Cream the butter and shortening together. Add the sugar gradually and beat until mixture is light and fluffy. Beat in the egg, vanilla and lemon rind.
3. Stir in the sifted flour mixture.
4. Chill the dough at least 1 hour.
5. Preheat oven to 325 degrees F. and lightly butter cookie sheets.
6. Working with one quarter of the dough at a time, roll out on lightly floured board to ¼ inch thickness and cut into heart, club, spade, and diamond shapes with a

special cutter. If desired, decorate cookies with chocolate shot, a piece of candied citrus peel, or colored sugar.

7. Bake on prepared cookie sheets 12 to 15 minutes, or until the edges of the cookies are light brown.

8. Let cool slightly before removing from cookie sheet.

BUTTER-NUT CRISPS
Makes about 45 cookies

Ease of preparation belies the elegance and distinction of this nut confection.

1 cup butter, softened
¾ cup sugar
1 egg, separated
1¾ cups flour
½ teaspoon salt
1 teaspoon vanilla
½ cup chopped walnuts

1. Preheat oven to 325 degrees F.
2. Cream the butter, then add the sugar, egg yolk, flour, salt, and vanilla.
3. Beat the egg white lightly.
4. Press the dough evenly into an ungreased jelly roll pan, then paint the surface with the egg white. Sprinkle the chopped nuts evenly on top.
5. Bake for about 40 minutes, or until the edges are light brown. Cut in bars while still warm.

CHOCOLATE ALMOND CRISPS
Makes about 45 cookies

If we had to choose the cookie most popular with our guests, this one would be a strong contender.

1 cup butter
½ cup packed light brown sugar
½ cup granulated sugar
1 egg yolk
1 teaspoon vanilla
1½ cups flour
Salt
8 ounces semi-sweet chocolate
¾ cup chopped toasted almonds

1. Preheat oven to 325 degrees F. and butter a jelly roll pan.
2. In a large bowl, cream together the butter and sugars until light and fluffy.
3. Add the egg yolk, vanilla, flour, and salt, and mix well. Spread evenly in buttered pan.
4. Bake about 30 minutes, or until golden brown. Remove from oven and cool 10 minutes.
5. While cookies are cooling, melt the chocolate in the top of a double boiler over hot, but not boiling, water. While the chocolate is still warm, spread it on top of the cookies and sprinkle the almonds over the chocolate. Let cool slightly, then cut in squares or diamonds.

CHOCOLATE-GLAZED TEA COOKIES
Makes about 60 cookies

Chocolate-glazed cookies are particularly fun to make, offering an opportunity to be imaginative with cookie-top design.

¾ cup butter, softened
⅔ cup sugar
½ teaspoon salt
2 egg yolks
2 teaspoons vanilla
2 cups sifted flour

Chocolate Glaze
4 ounces semi-sweet chocolate
2 tablespoons butter
1 tablespoon heavy cream

1. Cream the butter in a large mixing bowl. Gradually add the sugar and salt and beat until light and fluffy.
2. Add the egg yolks and vanilla and beat well.
3. Stir in the flour gradually, mixing until thoroughly blended and dough is smooth.
4. Divide dough into four parts and wrap each one separately. Refrigerate at least 4 hours.
5. Preheat oven to 350 degrees F. and butter cookie sheets.
6. Roll dough out on a floured board, one section at a

time; to ⅛-inch thickness. Cut circles, diamonds, or other shapes with cookie cutters. Place on cookie sheets.

7. Bake cookies about 10 minutes, or just until golden.

8. Remove cookies to a wire rack and cool completely.

9. In the top of a double boiler, melt the chocolate with the butter and cream over hot, not boiling, water. Remove from the heat and let cool a few minutes. Drizzle a design over the cookies, or frost one end. If glaze starts to harden, soften over hot water.

CHOCOLATE MERINGUE PUFFS
Makes 30 puffs

A light puff of chocolate, nuts, and melt-away meringue.

1 cup semi-sweet chocolate bits
2 egg whites
⅛ teaspoon salt
½ cup superfine sugar
½ teaspoon vinegar
1 teaspoon vanilla
½ cup chopped pecans

1. Preheat oven to 350 degrees F. and butter cookie sheets.

2. In the top of a double boiler, melt chocolate over hot water. Set aside.

3. In a medium bowl, beat egg whites with salt until foamy. Gradually beat in the sugar and continue beating until egg whites form stiff peaks. Beat in the vinegar and vanilla.

4. Fold in the chocolate and nuts.

5. Drop by heaping teaspoonfuls onto prepared cookie sheets.

6. Bake about 10 minutes. Remove at once and cool on racks. When completely cool, store in an airtight container.

CINNAMON APPLESAUCE SQUARES
Makes about 35 squares

The applesauce gives moisture and flavor to these spicy squares.

¾ cup butter, softened
1 cup firmly packed dark brown sugar
2 eggs
4 cups flour
3 teaspoons baking powder
½ teaspoon baking soda
1 teaspoon salt
1 teaspoon cinnamon
½ teaspoon allspice
Dash freshly grated nutmeg
2 cups applesauce
1½ cups chopped walnuts
1 cup raisins
Grated rind 1 lemon
Confectioners' sugar

1. Preheat oven to 350 degrees F. and butter an 11×14-inch pan.

2. Cream the butter and add the sugar gradually, beating until light and fluffy. Beat in the eggs one at a time.

3. Sift together the flour, baking powder, baking soda, salt, and spices.

4. To the batter, add the flour mixture alternately with the applesauce. Stir in the nuts, raisins, and lemon rind.

5. Bake for 30 minutes.

6. When cool, cut and sift with a light coating of confectioners' sugar.

COCONUT OATMEAL CRISPS
Makes 60 cookies

Here is the after-school snack favorite.

¾ cup butter, softened
1 cup firmly packed brown sugar
½ cup granulated sugar
1 egg
¼ cup orange juice
1 teaspoon vanilla
¾ cup flour
1 teaspoon salt
½ teaspoon baking soda
2½ cups regular oatmeal
1 cup shredded coconut
½ cup raisins
1 tablespoon grated orange rind

1. Preheat oven to 350 degrees F. and butter cookie sheets.

2. In a large bowl, cream the butter, then gradually add the brown and granulated sugars and beat well until light and fluffy. Beat in the egg, orange juice, and vanilla.

3. Sift together the flour, salt, and baking soda, and add to the creamed mixture. Blend well, then stir in the oatmeal, coconut, raisins, and orange rind.

4. Drop the batter by tablespoons onto prepared cookie sheets and bake for 12 to 15 minutes.

DATE NUT BARS
Makes about 20 bars

The contrasting texture of rich moist dates and crunchy walnuts makes this bar distinctive.

½ cup flour
½ teaspoon baking powder
½ teaspoon salt
2 eggs
½ cup sugar
1 teaspoon vanilla
Grated rind 1 lemon
1 cup coarsely chopped pitted dates
1½ cups coarsely chopped walnuts
Confectioners' sugar

1. Preheat oven to 350 degrees F. and lightly butter a 9-inch-square pan.

2. Sift flour, baking powder, and salt together and set aside.

3. Beat the eggs, then add the sugar slowly, beating until the mixture is light and fluffy.

4. Add the sifted flour and combine well. Add vanilla and lemon rind and stir in the dates and nuts.

5. Pour into prepared pan and bake 25 minutes.

6. Cool, then cut into bars and sift on a light coating of confectioners' sugar.

GOLDEN COCONUT DROPS
Makes 36 cookies

This is a soft moist drop cookie, full of chewy coconut and the tang of orange.

⅔ cup butter, softened
⅔ cup sugar
1 egg
2 cups grated coconut
1 cup flour
1 teaspoon vanilla
1 teaspoon grated orange rind

1. Preheat oven to 400 degrees F. and butter cookie sheets.

2. Cream the butter and gradually add the sugar, beating until light and fluffy. Add the egg and mix well.

3. Stir in the coconut, flour, vanilla, and orange rind.

4. Drop by teaspoonfuls on the cookie sheet and bake for 10 to 15 minutes, or until golden.

5. Cool slightly before removing cookies from sheet.

HERMITS
Makes 60 bars

A New England favorite, hermits date back to the days of
the clipper ships when housewives packed these spicy
long-lasting fruit bars for their seafaring husbands to take
on long voyages.

1 cup butter, softened
2 cups firmly packed brown sugar
3 eggs
3¼ cups flour
1 teaspoon baking powder
1 teaspoon baking soda
1 teaspoon cinnamon
1 teaspoon allspice
¼ cup honey
Grated rind 1 orange
1 teaspoon vanilla
½ cup chopped pitted dates
½ cup raisins

Frosting
3 tablespoons butter, softened
2 cups sifted confectioners' sugar
2 tablespoons heavy cream
1 teaspoon vanilla

1. Preheat oven to 350 degrees F. and butter a jelly
roll pan.

2. Cream the butter, then gradually add the sugar, beating until the mixture is light and fluffy.

3. Beat in the eggs one at a time.

4. Sift the flour, baking powder, baking soda, cinnamon, and allspice together and set aside.

5. Mix together the honey, orange rind, and vanilla.

6. To the creamed mixture, gradually add the honey alternately with the dry ingredients, and mix well.

7. Stir in the dates and raisins.

8. Pour the batter into the prepared pan and bake for 25 minutes, or until lightly browned. Let cool completely.

9. To frost, beat the butter, confectioners' sugar, cream, and vanilla together until smooth. Spread on the hermits and cut into bars.

KOULOURAKIA
Makes 4 dozen

An authentic recipe of a famous Greek cookie, rich but not too sweet, with aromatic spices and a distinctive shape.

1 cup butter, softened
¾ cup sugar
2 eggs
3 cups flour
¼ teaspoon baking soda

¼ teaspoon crushed sour salt ⎫
¼ teaspoon crushed *mahlepi* ⎬ If not available at a food specialty shop, substitute ¼ teaspoon almond extract and grated rind 1 lemon
¼ teaspoon crushed *mastieka* ⎭

Evaporated milk
Sesame seeds or chopped almonds

1. Cream the butter, then add the sugar gradually, beating until light and fluffy.

2. Beat in the eggs one at a time.

3. Stir in the flour and soda and mix well. Stir in the spices and refrigerate overnight in a covered bowl.

4. Preheat oven to 350 degrees F. and lightly oil cookie sheets.

5. Roll 1 tablespoon of dough at a time into 4-inch-long cylinders. Twist them to form a figure "8," and place them on the prepared cookie sheets.

6. Paint the formed cookies with evaporated milk and sprinkle the tops with sesame seeds or nuts.

7. Bake for 25 to 30 minutes.

8. Remove from sheets when cool.

MADELEINES
Makes 24 madeleines

Madeleines, those delectably light little spongecakes, have achieved both culinary recognition and literary renown through Marcel Proust. For the French author just one bite of the *"petite madeleine"* with tea evoked a rush of childhood memories that were later distilled in *Remembrance of Things Past*.

¾ cup sifted flour
½ teaspoon salt
3 eggs
1½ teaspoons vanilla
Grated rind 1 lemon
½ cup sugar
½ cup butter, melted and cooled
Confectioners' sugar

1. Preheat oven to 325 degrees F. and butter and flour enough madeleine pans to bake entire recipe of 24 at one time.

2. Sift flour and salt together.

3. Beat eggs, vanilla, and lemon rind until light and fluffy. Add sugar gradually and continue beating until mixture is thick and creamy.

4. Fold in the sifted flour. Add the melted butter and mix gently.

5. Fill the madeleine pans no more than two thirds full and bake for 15 minutes, or until lightly browned.

6. Cool a few minutes, then remove the madeleines carefully and cool completely on racks, fluted side up.

7. Sift on a light coating of confectioners' sugar and deliver the madeleines the same day since they are best enjoyed soon after baking.

MOLASSES SNAPS
Makes about 96 cookies

Crunchy, spicy, and sharp, an old-fashioned snap.

4 cups sifted flour
1¼ teaspoons baking soda
½ teaspoon salt
2 teaspoons ginger
1 teaspoon allspice
¾ cup butter, softened
1 cup granulated sugar
1 cup packed brown sugar
2 eggs
1 tablespoon lemon juice
1 teaspoon vanilla
⅔ cup molasses

1. Preheat oven to 325 degrees F. and lightly butter cookie sheets.

2. Sift the flour, soda, salt, ginger, and allspice together, and set aside.

3. Cream the butter and gradually add the white and brown sugars, beating until light and fluffy. Beat in the eggs, lemon juice, and vanilla, and stir in the molasses.

4. Stir in the flour and mix well. Refrigerate 2 hours.

5. Form into 1-inch balls and place 2 inches apart on the prepared cookie sheets. Bake for 15 minutes, or until the snaps have spread and are browned and crusty.

6. Cool before removing from cookie sheet.

OLD-FASHIONED SUGAR ROUNDS
Makes 4 to 5 dozen cookies

A lovely sugar cookie in a pretty shape.

2 cups flour, sifted
¾ teaspoon baking powder
½ cup butter, softened
1 cup sugar
1 egg yolk
¼ cup milk
Grated rind 1 lemon
1 teaspoon vanilla
1 egg white, slightly beaten with 1 tablespoon water
Colored sugar, for decorating
Cinnamon sugar, for decorating

1. Sift the flour and baking powder together and set aside.

2. Cream the butter, then add the sugar slowly and beat until mixture is light and fluffy.

3. Beat in the egg yolk.

4. Stir in the dry ingredients alternately with the milk, and add the lemon rind and vanilla.

5. Chill the dough at least 3 hours.

6. Preheat oven to 375 degrees F. and lightly butter cookie sheets.

7. Working with one quarter of the dough at a time, roll it out on a floured board to 1/4-inch thickness and cut into 2-inch circles or fluted rounds.

8. Place the rounds 1 1/2 inches apart on the prepared cookie sheets. Paint the tops of the cookies with the egg white and sprinkle with colored sugar or cinnamon sugar.

9. Bake 12 to 15 minutes, or until the cookies are slightly brown around the edges.

10. Cool before removing from cookie sheets.

PEANUT BUTTER COOKIES
Makes 8 dozen

2 3/4 cups flour
1 teaspoon baking soda
1 cup butter, softened
1 cup granulated sugar
1 cup packed light brown sugar
2 eggs
2 cups crunchy peanut butter
1 teaspoon vanilla
1/2 teaspoon salt
1/2 cup dry roast peanuts

1. Preheat oven to 350 degrees F. and butter cookie sheets.

2. Sift together the flour and baking soda.

3. Cream the butter, then gradually add the white and brown sugars, beating until the mixture is light and fluffy.

4. Beat in the eggs. Add the peanut butter, vanilla, salt, and sifted flour and mix well.

5. Form the dough into small balls and place on cookie sheets 2 inches apart. Flatten cookie slightly and gently press a peanut or two into the center of each cookie.

6. Bake for 20 minutes.

7. Cool before removing.

PECAN SNOWBALLS
Makes about 50 balls

Bite-size melt-in-the-mouth southern confections.

1 cup butter, softened
¼ cup granulated sugar
2 teaspoons vanilla
¼ teaspoon salt
2 cups flour
2 cups finely chopped pecans
Confectioners' sugar

1. Cream butter well. Gradually add the granulated sugar and beat until light and fluffy. Add the vanilla and salt.

2. Stir in the flour and nuts and mix until well blended.

3. Form the dough into a large ball and wrap in wax paper. Refrigerate at least an hour.

4. Preheat oven to 375 degrees F.

5. Shape dough into 1-inch balls and place on ungreased baking sheets about 1 inch apart.

6. Bake balls 15 minutes, or until the balls are cooked but not yet brown.

7. Remove from oven and let cool a few minutes on baking sheets. While still warm, roll the balls in confectioners' sugar to coat. Cool completely on wire racks and store in airtight containers.

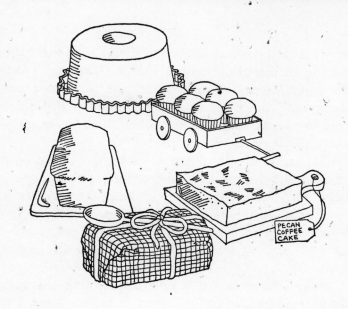

10

The Cake Plate

CAKES ARE TRADITIONAL OFFERINGS for friends, neighbors, church suppers, and almost any gift-giving occasion —and with good reason. They travel well, are good to look at, and better to eat.

This chapter offers a wide selection of cakes—chocolate, pound, spice, fruit nut, coffee cakes, health specialties. They come in squares, loaves, rings, layers, cupcakes, upside down and right side up. These cakes have good keeping qualities and all can be frozen. Protect all of them

with plastic wrap for maximum freshness. The two frosted
cakes included here—Favorite Fudge Cake and Frosted
Brownie Cupcakes—require additional care; to prevent
sticking, chill the frosted cakes thoroughly, then enclose
loosely in plastic wrap or package under glass or plastic
domes on trays or cheese boards.

Packaging is usually determined by the shape of the
cake, so look for unusual round, square, and oblong containers. Trays and baskets of all kinds and shapes are
always useful, as are one-of-a-kind plates.

Round cakes fit nicely into ceramic or metal quiche
pans, hatboxes, or, for special display, in a circular terrarium.

A square cheese board is superb for toting the upside
down cake and pecan coffee cake; if it has no dome, wrap
and tie with brightly colored yarn.

Wrap loaf cakes in colorful dish towels and tie on a
wooden spoon, whisk, or other utensil. Present one loaf
cake on a bread board, shiny baking sheet, or Lucite cutting board.

Cupcakes, of course, are children's favorites, so pack
the gingerbread in a cowboy's hat, and line the frosted
brownie cupcakes up in a toy wagon.

FAVORITE FUDGE CAKE
Makes 9-inch round two-layer cake

4 ounces baking chocolate
1 cup boiling water
½ cup butter, softened
1 cup packed brown sugar
1 cup granulated sugar
3 eggs, separated
1 teaspoon vanilla
2¼ cups sifted flour
1¼ teaspoons baking soda
½ teaspoon salt
1 cup sour cream

Frosting
4 tablespoons butter, softened
2½ cups sifted confectioners' sugar
4 ounces baking chocolate, melted
1 teaspoon vanilla
4 tablespoons black coffee
2 egg yolks

1. Preheat oven to 350 degrees F. and line the bottoms of two round 9-inch layer pans with wax paper.
2. Melt chocolate in boiling water, and let cool.
3. In a large bowl, cream the butter well. Gradually add the brown sugar and ½ cup of the granulated sugar and continue beating until light and fluffy.
4. Beat in the egg yolks one at a time. Add vanilla.
5. Sift together the flour, baking soda, and salt, and add to the creamed mixture alternately with the sour cream.
6. Add the chocolate and mix thoroughly.

7. In a small bowl, beat the egg whites until soft peaks form. Gradually add the remaining ½ cup sugar and continue beating until egg whites are stiff.

8. Fold egg whites into rest of batter and pour into prepared pans. Bake 40 to 45 minutes.

9. Let cake cool slightly, then turn out layers on cake rack. Peel off paper and cool completely.

10. To make the frosting, cream the butter and beat in the sugar, melted chocolate, vanilla, coffee, and egg yolks to a smooth spreading consistency.

11. Frost cake when completely cool. Chill well before wrapping.

A NOTE To prevent the frosting from sticking to the package, chill cake before unwrapping.

SWEET STANLEY'S CHOCOLATE CHIP CAKE
Makes one 9-inch ring

Our search for the perfect chocolate chip cake led us to Stanley Schear, the delightful proprietor of Jespersen's Bakery in Scarsdale, who helped us develop this chocolate-studded pound cake.

2 cups sifted cake flour
½ teaspoon salt
½ teaspoon baking powder
1 cup butter, softened
1 cup sugar
6 eggs, separated and at room temperature
2 teaspoons vanilla
10 ounces semi-sweet baking chocolate, chopped into tiny
    pieces about ⅛ inch in size

1. Preheat oven to 325 degrees F. and butter and flour a 9-inch ring pan.

2. Sift together the flour, salt, and baking powder and set aside.

3. In a large bowl, cream the butter well. Gradually add ½ cup of the sugar and continue beating until mixture is light and fluffy.

4. Beat in the egg yolks one at a time. Add vanilla.

5. Stir in the dry ingredients.

6. Beat the egg whites until stiff. Gradually beat in the remaining ½ cup of sugar. Fold the egg whites into the cake batter.

7. Fold the chocolate pieces into the batter.

8. Pour batter into prepared pan and bake for 60 to 80 minutes, or until the top is nicely browned and cake pulls away from the edge of the pan. Let cool 15 minutes and remove to cake rack to complete cooling.

CHOCOLATE PECAN UPSIDE DOWN CAKE
Makes one 9-inch square

Here is an unusual upside down cake, rich and moist with a candied-nut topping.

3 ounces baking chocolate
2 cups sifted flour
¾ teaspoon baking soda
¾ teaspoon salt
½ cup shortening
1½ cups sugar
3 eggs

¾ cup sour cream
1½ teaspoons vanilla
¼ cup butter, melted
⅓ cup packed brown sugar
1 cup coarsely chopped pecans
¾ cup light corn syrup

1. Preheat oven to 350 degrees F.
2. Melt the chocolate in top of double boiler over hot but not boiling water.
3. Sift together the flour, baking soda, and salt, then set aside.
4. Cream the shortening in a large bowl. Gradually add the sugar and beat until light and fluffy. Beat in the eggs one at a time. Stir in the melted chocolate.
5. Combine the sour cream and vanilla, and add to the chocolate mixture alternately with the sifted flour. Mix well.
6. In a small bowl, combine the butter, sugar, nuts, and corn syrup and spread evenly in the bottom of a 9-inch square baking pan. Pour in the chocolate cake batter and bake for 60 to 65 minutes.
7. Turn cake out immediately on a cake rack.

FROSTED BROWNIE CUPCAKES
Makes 24 cupcakes

A combination of the best of all possible worlds—fudge brownies and cupcakes.

4 ounces unsweetened chocolate
1 cup butter
1½ cups chopped pecans
1¾ cups sugar
1 cup flour
4 eggs
1 teaspoon vanilla

Frosting
1 egg
3 tablespoons milk
1 cup sugar
2 tablespoons cocoa
2 tablespoons butter
½ teaspoon vanilla
24 candy-covered chocolate dots, for decorating

1. Preheat oven to 325 degrees F.
2. In a heavy saucepan, melt the chocolate and butter over low heat. Add nuts and stir until they are coated.
3. In a mixing bowl, combine the sugar, flour, eggs, and vanilla. Mix well until blended but do not beat.
4. Add the chocolate mixture to the mixing bowl and stir in carefully.
5. Pour batter into paper or foil baking cups and bake for 30 minutes. Cool.
6. For the frosting, beat egg in a saucepan, then stir in milk. Add the sugar, cocoa, and butter. Place the saucepan over medium heat, bring the mixture to a boil, and continue cooking for 5 minutes. Remove from heat and let cool.
7. Add vanilla and beat until creamy.
8. Frost cupcakes when they are cool and decorate each

with a candy-covered chocolate dot. Refrigerate before
wrapping.

A NOTE   To prevent the frosting from sticking to the
package, chill before unwrapping.

SPICY JAM CAKE
Makes one 10-inch tube cake

In every way, an unusual cake, from the almond-coated
crust to the spicy jam marbling.

½ cup shaved unblanched almonds
1 cup raspberry jam
2 tablespoons Grand Marnier
¾ cup butter, softened
2 cups sugar
5 eggs
3 cups flour, sifted
1½ teaspoons baking soda
½ teaspoon salt
1 teaspoon ginger
1 cup sour cream
Grated rind 1 orange
1 teaspoon vanilla
Superfine sugar

   1. Preheat oven to 350 degrees F., butter a 10-inch
tube pan well, and coat with almonds.
   2. Combine the jam and liqueur and set aside.

3. In a large bowl, cream the butter well. Gradually add the sugar, beating until mixture is light and fluffy.

4. Beat in the eggs one at a time.

5. Sift together the flour, baking soda, salt, and ginger, and add to the creamed mixture alternately with the sour cream.

6. Stir in the orange rind and vanilla, mixing well, then lightly fold in the jam mixture just to streak the batter.

7. Pour batter into prepared pan and bake 50 to 60 minutes, or until cake is golden.

8. Cool cake slightly, then turn out on plate. When thoroughly cool, dust the top with superfine sugar.

TRADITIONAL POUND CAKE
Makes one 10-inch tube cake

2 cups butter, softened
2 cups sugar
12 eggs, separated
2 teaspoons vanilla
Grated rind 1 lemon
4 cups sifted cake flour
1 teaspoon baking powder
Confectioners' sugar

1. Preheat oven to 325 degrees F. and butter and flour a 10-inch tube pan.

2. Cream the butter well. Gradually add 1 cup of the sugar and beat until light and fluffy.

3. Beat in the egg yolks a few at a time. Add vanilla and lemon rind.

4. Beat the egg whites until stiff but not dry. Gradually add remaining cup of sugar and beat until completely absorbed.

5. Sift the flour and baking powder together and fold gently into the rest of the batter alternately with the beaten egg whites.

6. Pour batter into prepared pan and bake about 1 hour, or until cake is golden.

7. When cake is completely cool, dust the top with sifted confectioners' sugar.

GINGERBREAD CUPCAKES
Makes 12 cupcakes

An old favorite, made more flavorful by the addition of orange zest, presented in cupcake form.

½ cup butter
1 cup molasses
2½ cups flour
1 teaspoon baking soda
¼ teaspoon salt
1 teaspoon ginger
1 teaspoon cinnamon
¼ teaspoon allspice
1 cup sour cream
Grated rind 1 orange

1. Preheat oven to 350 degrees F.

2. In a small saucepan, melt the butter and stir in the molasses.

3. Sift together the flour, baking soda, salt, ginger, cinnamon, and allspice. Stir in the butter-molasses mixture. Add the sour cream and orange rind and combine well.

4. Pour the batter into paper or foil baking cups and bake 30 minutes, or until inserted cake tester comes out clean.

A NOTE Serve warm with whipped cream or hard sauce.

AUTUMN APPLESAUCE CAKE
Makes 1 bundt cake

A spicy, moist, fruit-filled cake in a lovely bundt form.

2 cups chopped walnuts
1 cup chopped dates
1 cup currants
Grated rind 1 lemon
3 cups sifted flour
½ cup butter, softened
¾ cup sugar
2 eggs
2 teaspoons baking soda
2 teaspoons cinnamon
1 teaspoon allspice
½ teaspoon salt
2 cups applesauce
Confectioners' sugar

1. Preheat oven to 350 degrees F. and butter a bundt pan.

2. In a medium bowl, combine the nuts, dates, currants, and lemon rind with ½ cup of the flour. Set mixture aside.

3. In a large bowl, cream the butter well. Gradually add the sugar and beat until mixture is light and fluffy.

4. Beat in the eggs one at a time.

5. Sift together the remaining 2½ cups flour, baking soda, cinnamon, allspice, and salt. Add them to the creamed mixture alternately with the applesauce.

6. Stir in the walnuts, dates, currants, and lemon rind.

7. Pour the batter into prepared pan and bake 50 to 60 minutes, or until inserted cake tester comes out clean.

8. Cool cake slightly, then turn out on plate. When completely cool, dust the top with sifted confectioners' sugar.

SPICY BANANA NUT LOAF
Makes 1 loaf

Candied ginger brings a sharp accent to the mellow taste of banana.

6 tablespoons butter, softened
¾ cup sugar
2 eggs
¼ cup milk
1¾ cups flour
½ teaspoon baking soda
1½ teaspoons baking powder
½ teaspoon salt

1 cup mashed bananas
Grated rind 1 lemon
2 tablespoons finely chopped candied ginger
½ cup chopped walnuts

1. Preheat oven to 350 degrees F. and butter a 9×5-inch loaf pan.
2. In a large bowl, cream butter well. Gradually add the sugar, beating until mixture is light and fluffy.
3. Beat in the eggs one at a time. Add milk.
4. Sift together the flour, baking soda, baking powder, and salt, and stir into the creamed mixture.
5. Stir in the bananas, lemon rind, ginger, and nuts.
6. Pour batter into prepared pan and bake for 1 hour, or until inserted cake tester comes out clean. Cool in pan 15 minutes, then remove and cool completely on cake rack. Wrap tightly and refrigerate for 24 hours to ripen flavor.

CALIFORNIA FRUITCAKE
Makes 1 bundt cake

An enormously popular cream cheese pound cake filled with the fruits and flavors of California.

1 cup raisins
4 tablespoons port wine
½ cup chopped dates
3 cups self-rising flour
1 cup butter, softened
1 cup cream cheese, softened

2½ cups sugar
5 eggs
Grated rind 1 navel orange
Grated rind 1 lemon
1 cup chopped walnuts
½ cup orange juice

1. Preheat oven to 350 degrees F. and butter a bundt pan.
2. Soak the raisins in the wine, and set aside.
3. Toss the dates in 2 tablespoons of the flour and set aside.
4. Cream the butter and cream cheese well. Gradually add 2 cups of the sugar and beat until mixture is light and fluffy.
5. Beat in the eggs one at a time.
6. Sift the remaining flour and add to the batter.
7. Stir in the raisins and wine, floured dates, grated orange and lemon rinds, and walnuts.
8. Pour batter into prepared pan and bake for 50 to 60 minutes, or until cake is golden.
9. Mix the orange juice and remaining ½ cup of sugar together and simmer for 5 minutes. Spoon over the hot cake while it is still in the pan. Remove cake from the pan when completely cool.

LEMON LOAF
Makes 1 loaf

A tangy teatime loaf, kept moist by a post-baking lemon-juice soak.

⅓ cup butter, softened
1¼ cups sugar
2 eggs
¼ teaspoon lemon extract
1½ cups sifted flour
1 teaspoon baking powder
1 teaspoon salt
½ cup milk
¾ cup chopped walnuts
Grated rind 1 lemon
Juice 1 lemon

1. Preheat oven to 350 degrees F. and butter a 9×5-inch loaf pan.

2. In a large bowl, cream the butter and 1 cup of the sugar.

3. Beat in the eggs one at a time, and add the lemon extract.

4. Sift the flour, baking powder, and salt together.

5. Add the sifted ingredients to the creamed mixture alternately with the milk. Stir in the nuts and lemon rind.

6. Pour batter into prepared pan and bake for 1 hour, or until cake is golden.

7. Simmer the lemon juice with the remaining ¼ cup of sugar for 10 minutes. Pour over the hot cake. Cool cake for 15 minutes in pan, then cool completely on cake rack.

HAWAIIAN NUT LOAF
Makes 2 loaves

For a complete Hawaiian treat, serve this lightly sweetened loaf with Kona coffee.

½ cup butter, softened
1½ cups sugar
2 eggs
1 teaspoon vanilla
4 cups sifted flour
2 teaspoons baking powder
1 teaspoon baking soda
1 teaspoon salt
1 cup chopped macadamia nuts
2 cups canned crushed pineapple
Grated rind 1 lemon
Grated rind 1 orange

1. Preheat oven to 350 degrees F. and butter two 9×5-inch loaf pans.

2. In a large bowl, cream the butter well. Gradually add the sugar, beating until light and fluffy.

3. Beat in the eggs one at a time. Add the vanilla.

4. Sift together the flour, baking powder, baking soda, and salt, then stir in the chopped nuts and coat them well.

5. To the creamed mixture, add half the sifted flour, stirring until thoroughly moistened, then the crushed pineapple and lemon and orange rinds, then the remaining flour. Mix until well blended.

6. Pour batter into prepared loaf pans and bake for 50 to 60 minutes, or until loaves are golden. Cool 15 minutes in pan, then cool completely on cake rack. Wrap tightly and store in refrigerator for 24 hours to ripen flavor.

LIGHT FRUITCAKE
Makes one 10-inch tube pan

A beautifully decorated cake for festive occasions, studded with bright bits of cherries and pineapple.

1 cup slivered almonds	4 eggs
1 cup white raisins	1 teaspoon vanilla
1 cup grated coconut	3½ cups flour
1 cup quartered red candied cherries	1 teaspoon baking powder
1 cup diced candied pineapple	1 teaspoon baking soda
Grated rind 1 lemon	½ teaspoon salt
Grated rind 1 orange	¼ cup orange juice
1 cup butter, softened	¼ cup lemon juice
2 cups sugar	Honey
	Whole blanched almonds
	Whole candied cherries

1. Preheat oven to 300 degrees F., butter a 10-inch tube pan and line with buttered wax paper.

2. In a bowl, toss together the almonds, raisins, coconut, candied cherries and pineapple, and lemon and orange rinds until well combined. Set aside.

3. In a large bowl, cream the butter well. Gradually add the sugar and continue beating until light and fluffy.

4. Beat in the eggs one at a time. Add vanilla.

5. Sift together the flour, baking powder, soda, and salt, and add them to the creamed mixture alternately with the orange and lemon juices. Stir the fruit into the cake batter.

6. Pour batter into the prepared pan and bake for 2 hours, or until the cake is golden.

7. Cool slightly, then remove to cake rack. While cake is still cooling, brush top with honey and decorate with whole blanched almonds and whole candied cherries to form daisies. Use the almonds to form the petals and the cherries for the centers.

8. When cake is completely cool, store in a plastic bag.

LINZERTORTE
Makes one 9-inch torte

This open raspberry jam pie with its rich and crumbly crust is a superb delicacy from Austria.

¾ cup butter
1¼ cups flour, sifted
⅔ cup sugar
1¼ cups ground unblanched almonds
1 egg
Grated rind 1 lemon
½ teaspoon allspice
¾ cup raspberry jam
¼ cup shaved unblanched almonds

1. Preheat oven to 350 degrees F. and lightly butter a 9-inch round springform pan or a layer cake pan with removable bottom.

2. Cut the butter into the flour.

3. Add the sugar, ground nuts, egg, lemon rind, and allspice, and knead together.

4. Refrigerate one third of the dough while you press the remaining two thirds evenly into the prepared pan, covering the bottom and pressing it up the sides about 1½ inches.

5. Bake 20 minutes and let cool.

6. Pour the jam into the baked shell.

7. Form the remaining chilled dough into strips to make a lattice over the jam.

8. Bake 30 to 40 minutes on lower shelf of oven.

9. Sprinkle with shaved almonds and cool slightly before removing sides of the pan. Then cool completely.

ORANGE RUM CAKE
Makes one 10-inch tube cake

Hot rum sauce spooned over this orange-nut cake lends a sophisticated touch.

1 cup butter, softened
1½ cups sugar
3 eggs
Grated rind 1 orange
Grated rind 1 lemon
2½ cups flour, sifted
2 teaspoons baking powder
1 teaspoon baking soda
½ teaspoon salt
1 cup buttermilk
1 cup chopped walnuts

Sauce
Juice 1 orange
Juice 1 lemon
¾ cup sugar
¼ cup rum

1. Preheat oven to 350 degrees F. and butter a 10-inch tube pan.

2. In a large bowl, cream the butter well. Gradually add the sugar, beating until mixture is light and fluffy.

3. Beat in the eggs one at a time. Add the orange and lemon rind.

4. Sift together the flour, baking powder, baking soda, and salt, and add to the creamed mixture alternately with the buttermilk.

5. Fold the nuts into the batter.

6. Pour the batter into the prepared tube pan and bake for 50 to 60 minutes, or until inserted cake tester comes out clean.

7. In a saucepan, combine the orange juice, lemon juice, sugar, and rum for the sauce and bring to a boil. Simmer 10 minutes.

8. When cake is done, let it cool slightly, then turn it out on a plate. Spoon the hot sauce over the warm cake.

PECAN COFFEE CAKE
Makes one 9-inch square cake

A light cake with a marvelous buttery nut topping.

1½ cups flour
½ teaspoon salt
2 teaspoons baking powder
2 eggs, separated
½ cup milk
2 teaspoons vanilla
⅓ cup butter, softened
1 cup sugar

Topping
¼ cup sugar
½ cup coarsely chopped pecans
Dash cinnamon
¼ cup butter, melted

1. Preheat oven to 350 degrees F. and butter and flour a 9-inch square pan.
2. Sift flour, salt, and baking powder together, and set aside.
3. Beat egg yolks and add milk and vanilla. Set aside.
4. In a large mixing bowl, cream the butter and sugar, and alternately add the wet and dry ingredients, mixing well.
5. Beat the egg whites until stiff, then fold into the batter and pour batter into prepared pan.
6. For the topping, mix together the sugar, nuts, and cinnamon, and sprinkle over the batter. Then drizzle the melted butter over the topping.
7. Bake for 30 minutes, or until cake is golden.

SOUR CREAM COFFEE CAKE
Makes one 9-inch ring

A moist rich coffee cake with a spicy nut filling.

Filling
½ cup sugar
1 teaspoon cinnamon
¾ cup chopped pecans

Cake
½ cup butter, softened
1 cup sugar
2 eggs
2 cups flour
1 teaspoon baking soda
1½ teaspoons baking powder
⅛ teaspoon salt
1 cup sour cream
1 teaspoon vanilla

1. Preheat oven to 350 degrees F. and butter a 9-inch springform tube pan.
2. In a small bowl, combine the sugar, cinnamon, and nuts for the filling. Set aside.
3. In a large bowl, cream the butter well. Gradually add the sugar, beating until light and fluffy.
4. Beat in the eggs one at a time.
5. Sift the flour, baking soda, baking powder, and salt

together, and add them to the creamed mixture alternately with the sour cream. Stir in the vanilla.

6. Pour half the batter into the prepared pan and top with half the filling mixture. Pour over the remaining batter and top with the remaining filling.

7. Bake for 40 minutes, or until inserted cake tester comes out clean.

8. Cool slightly and remove from pan.

YOGURT POUND CAKE
Makes one 10-inch tube cake

The tang of lemon and yogurt and the crunch of almonds in an unusual and giftworthy pound cake.

½ cup slivered almonds
1 cup butter, softened
2 cups sugar
5 eggs
Grated rind 2 lemons
1 teaspoon vanilla
3 cups sifted flour
1 teaspoon baking powder
1 teaspoon baking soda
1 cup yogurt
Confectioners' sugar

1. Preheat oven to 350 degrees F. and butter a 10-inch tube pan. Sprinkle the pan with the slivered almonds.

2. Cream the butter well. Gradually add the sugar and continue beating until mixture is light and fluffy.

3. Beat in the eggs one at a time. Add the lemon rind and vanilla.

4. Sift together the flour, baking powder, and baking soda and add to the creamed mixture alternately with the yogurt.

5. Pour batter into prepared pan and bake 70 minutes, or until cake is golden.

6. Let cake cool slightly, then turn out onto plate. When thoroughly cool, dust with sifted confectioners' sugar.

SPICY HEALTH LOAF
Makes 1 loaf

A spicy cake to please natural-food fans.

2½ cups whole wheat flour
3 teaspoons baking powder
½ teaspoon baking soda
½ cup powdered skim milk
1 cup brown sugar
1 teaspoon cinnamon
1 teaspoon allspice
½ teaspoon freshly grated nutmeg
Grated rind 1 orange
4 eggs
⅔ cup corn oil
1 cup buttermilk

1. Preheat oven to 350 degrees F. and butter a 9×5-inch loaf pan.

2. Into a large mixing bowl, sift together the flour, baking powder, baking soda, powdered skim milk, brown sugar, cinnamon, allspice, and nutmeg. Add the orange rind.

3. Into the center of these dry ingredients, add the eggs, corn oil, and buttermilk. Mix well.

4. Pour batter into prepared pan and bake 45 to 50 minutes, or until inserted cake tester comes out clean.

CARROT NUT RING
Makes one 10-inch tube cake

Nutritious raisins and carrots add moisture and texture to a spicy nut cake.

2 cups sugar
1½ cups corn oil
3 cups unbleached white flour
3 teaspoons baking powder
½ teaspoon baking soda
¼ teaspoon salt
1 teaspoon cinnamon
½ teaspoon freshly grated nutmeg
4 eggs
1 cup chopped walnuts
1 cup raisins
2 cups peeled and coarsely grated carrots
Confectioners' sugar

1. Preheat oven to 350 degrees F. and butter a 10-inch tube pan.

2. In a large mixing bowl, beat the sugar into the oil.

3. Sift together the flour, baking powder, baking soda, salt, cinnamon, and nutmeg, and add them to the oil and sugar mixture alternately with the eggs.

4. Stir in the nuts, raisins, and carrots.

5. Pour batter into prepared pan and bake 50 to 60 minutes, or until inserted cake tester comes out clean.

6. Cool slightly, then turn out on plate. When completely cool, dust top with sifted confectioners' sugar.

11

The Candy Jar

IF YOU ASSUME that one never outgrows a love for candy,
that a childhood passion for homemade fudge subsides
into a more restrained appreciation of Parisian truffles,
you'll never wonder what to bring a hostess who seems to
have everything.

Candy making can be a delightful family enterprise, a
special treat for youngsters to make as well as to receive.
The candy recipes offered here are carefully selected for
home production. They keep best when stored airtight

in a cool place. When well wrapped, fudge-type candy keeps fresh up to 1 week, other candy 2 to 3 weeks. Whenever possible, candy should be protected by plastic wrap or colored cellophane.

Packaging candy as gifts immediately calls to mind containers that will delight children, if only because youngsters are likely to get their hands on it first anyway. The possibilities are as intriguing as a toy store:

Pack nut brittle in a set of stacking blocks.

Cluster lollipops in a pencil holder or mug.

Pile chocolate mint or nut bark in a watering can.

Stuff an assortment of peanut, raisin, and popcorn clusters in a small fish tank.

Make a delivery of fudge and penuche in a toy dump truck.

Stow caramel nut chews and chocolate almond crunch in a beach pail.

Fill the drawers of a miniature jewelry chest with butterscotch thins and candied orange peel.

Heap a doctor's bag with chocolate caramel butterflies and a bongo drum with pralines.

Candy for more sophisticated tastes may be presented with more elegance. For example, pile a pewter tankard or porcelain cachepot high with creamy mint balls. Group apricot balls, Viennese nut balls, and Parisian truffles in the three gleaming tiers of a glass stack dish. Deposit a collection of crystal mint coins in an oversize brandy snifter or a Lucite recipe box.

NEVER-FAIL FUDGE
Makes sixty-four 1-inch squares

For most children, making fudge is an introduction to the pleasures of cooking and gift-giving. This recipe recalls early fudge-stirring days.

2 cups sugar
¼ cup corn syrup
¾ cup milk
2 ounces baking chocolate
2 tablespoons butter
1 teaspoon vanilla
1 cup chopped walnuts

1. Butter an 8-inch square pan.
2. In a heavy 3-quart saucepan, mix the sugar, corn syrup, milk, and baking chocolate over low heat, stirring together carefully until the chocolate melts and the mixture begins to boil. Insert a candy thermometer and cook without stirring until the temperature reaches 238 degrees F.
3. Remove from heat and add the butter and vanilla. Cool to lukewarm, or 110 degrees F.
4. Add the nuts and beat with a wooden spoon until the mixture thickens and just begins to lose its gloss. Pour at once into prepared pan and score into 1-inch squares.
5. Wrap pieces individually in plastic and keep in a cool place in a tightly capped container.

NUT PENUCHE
Makes 1½ pounds

Nut penuche is old-fashioned brown sugar fudge studded with walnuts.

1 pound light brown sugar (2¼ cups packed)
¾ cup light cream
⅛ teaspoon salt
3 tablespoons light corn syrup
3 tablespoons butter
1 teaspoon vanilla
½ cup broken walnuts

1. Butter an 8-inch square pan.
2. In a heavy saucepan, combine the sugar, cream, salt, and corn syrup, and cook over medium heat, stirring until the sugar dissolves. When mixture comes to a boil, insert a candy thermometer and cook without stirring until the temperature reaches 238 degrees F. Remove from heat.
3. Without stirring, add the butter and let cool to lukewarm, 110 degrees F.
4. Stir in the vanilla and nuts, and beat the mixture with a wooden spoon until it thickens and just begins to lose its gloss. Pour at once into prepared pan and score into 1-inch squares.
5. When cool, cut and wrap squares individually in plastic wrap. Store in an airtight container in a cool place.

PRALINES
Makes 1½ pounds

A mouth-watering confection from New Orleans, pralines are brown-sugar fudge patties studded with pecans.

1 cup granulated sugar
1 cup packed light brown sugar
½ cup light cream
¼ cup butter
2 cups coarsely chopped pecans
1 teaspoon vanilla

1. In a heavy saucepan, mix the granulated and brown sugars, cream, and butter, and stir over low heat until the sugars dissolve and mixture comes to a boil.
2. Insert candy thermometer and cook at a slow boil, stirring constantly until the temperature registers 238 degrees F. Remove from heat.
3. When mixture is lukewarm, add nuts and vanilla.
4. Drop by large spoonfuls onto a sheet of buttered wax paper to form patties.
5. Package patties individually in clear plastic wrap and store in a tightly covered container in a cool place.

OLD-FASHIONED PEANUT BRITTLE
Makes 1 pound

A simple, clear, crisp brittle that doesn't require a candy thermometer.

2 cups sugar
1 cup dry roast peanuts

1. Oil a cookie sheet lightly.
2. In a large heavy skillet, stir the sugar over medium heat until it dissolves and becomes a caramel-colored syrup. Guard against burning.
3. Remove pan from heat and quickly stir in the nuts.
4. Pour immediately on the prepared cookie sheet, spreading the brittle as thin as you wish.
5. Cool and break into pieces. Keep in a tightly covered container in a cool place.

MIXED NUT BRITTLE
Makes 2¼ pounds

Use any of your favorite nuts in this traditional brittle recipe.

2 cups granulated sugar
1 cup packed brown sugar
½ cup light corn syrup

½ cup water
2 tablespoons butter, softened
2 cups mixed nuts
1 teaspoon baking soda
½ teaspoon salt

1. Lightly oil a cookie sheet.
2. In a large heavy saucepan, cook the granulated sugar, brown sugar, corn syrup, and water over low heat, stirring constantly until the sugars dissolve. When the syrup comes to a boil, insert a candy thermometer and cook over medium high heat without stirring until the temperature reaches 300 degrees F.
3. Remove saucepan from heat and lightly stir in butter, nuts, baking soda, and salt.
4. Pour brittle immediately onto the prepared cookie sheet and spread out, stretching the candy out thin as soon as it is cool enough to handle.
5. When cool, break into pieces and store in an airtight container in a cool place.

BUTTERSCOTCH THINS
Makes about sixty 1½-inch rounds

Old-fashioned golden coins with the flavor of butter and brown sugar.

1 cup granulated sugar
1 cup packed brown sugar
½ cup light corn syrup
½ cup butter
4 tablespoons water
2 tablespoons vinegar

1. Lightly oil cookie sheets.
2. Combine all the ingredients in a heavy saucepan. Cook over medium heat, stirring until the sugar is dissolved and mixture comes to a boil.
3. Insert a candy thermometer and cook without stirring until the temperature reaches 300 degrees F.
4. Remove from heat and drop by teaspoonfuls on prepared cookie sheets to form 1½-inch rounds. If the candy starts to harden before you are finished, put the saucepan in a pan of hot water until the consistency improves.
5. Store in an airtight container in a cool place.

A NOTE   For a delicious topping, crush butterscotch thins and sprinkle over ice cream.

CRYSTAL MINT COINS
Makes 24 quarter-size rounds

A refreshing after-dinner treat.

1 cup sugar
⅓ cup water
⅓ cup light corn syrup
3 drops oil of peppermint
6 drops green food coloring
3 drops blue food coloring

1. Lightly oil a cookie sheet.
2. Combine the sugar and water in a heavy saucepan. Add the corn syrup and cook over medium heat, stirring until the sugar is dissolved and the mixture starts to boil.

Wipe the sugar crystals from the sides of the pan with a brush or damp cloth.

3. When the mixture comes to a boil, insert a candy thermometer and cook without stirring until the temperature reaches 290 degrees F.

4. Remove pan from heat and gently stir in the oil of peppermint and food coloring.

5. Immediately drop small teaspoonfuls onto prepared cookie sheet to form quarter-size drops. Work quickly, but if candy hardens, put the saucepan in a pan of hot water until consistency improves.

6. When cool, package coins individually in plastic wrap and keep in a cool dry place.

A NOTE For an elegant dessert, crush a few mint coins and sprinkle over vanilla ice cream served with a dash of crème de menthe.

LOLLIPOPS
Makes twelve 2-inch lollipops

2 cups sugar
1 cup water
1 cup light corn syrup
1 teaspoon powdered citric acid
1 teaspoon oil of orange, lemon, or lime
8 to 10 drops orange, yellow, or green food coloring

1. Lightly oil a cookie sheet.
2. Combine the sugar and water in a heavy saucepan. Add the corn syrup and cook over medium heat, stirring

until the sugar is dissolved and the mixture starts to boil. Wipe the sugar crystals from the sides of the pan with a brush or damp cloth.

3. When the mixture comes to a boil, insert a candy thermometer and cook without stirring until the temperature reaches 290 degrees F.

4. Remove pan from heat and stir in the citric acid and the flavoring oil. Stir just until well blended. Add the food coloring and stir just until color is evenly distributed throughout the candy.

5. On prepared cookie sheet, pour round patties about 2 inches in diameter and press a lollipop stick into each one. Let cool slightly and loosen from pan while still warm.

6. When cool, package individually in plastic wrap and store in cool, dry place.

CANDIED ORANGE PEEL
Makes 2 cups

Give this to a friend who makes fruitcakes, decorates cookies, or who just likes to nibble on this not-too-sweet treat.

5 navel oranges
2½ cups sugar
¾ cup water

1. Carefully peel the oranges, removing as much of the white membrane as possible from the peel. Cut the peel into strips about 1½ to 2 inches long, and ¼ inch wide.

2. Place peel in a saucepan, cover with cold water, and bring to a boil. Cook for 15 minutes, then drain water and rinse thoroughly. Repeat this process three more times.

3. In a medium saucepan, mix 2 cups of the sugar with the water and bring to a boil. When the sugar is dissolved, reduce the heat and add the peel, cooking it slowly until it looks translucent. Watch carefully as the liquid is reduced and the sugar is absorbed to avoid burning.

4. Spread remaining sugar on a piece of wax paper and roll each piece of peel until thoroughly coated with sugar. Dry peel on wire rack. Store in an airtight container.

APRICOT BALLS
Makes 50 bite-size balls

This confection ages beautifully, so keep it on hand for gift-giving all year long.

1½ cups dried apricots
1 cup pecans
1 cup (3½-ounce can) flaked coconut
3 tablespoons orange juice
1 teaspoon grated orange rind
Superfine sugar

1. Steam apricots for 15 minutes in top of a double boiler.

2. Process nuts a few at a time in blender until finely chopped. Remove to a large mixing bowl.

3. Process coconut in blender. Add to chopped nuts.

4. Process apricots in blender until finely chopped but not puréed. Work with one third of the apricots at a time and use 1 tablespoon of orange juice as liquid for each batch.

5. Add apricot mixture to the mixing bowl and then the orange rind. Combine all ingredients well and shape into bite-size balls. Roll in sugar.

6. Let the apricot balls dry overnight, then store in an airtight container in the refrigerator.

RUM RAISIN DROPS
Makes about 1 pound

2 cups golden raisins
¼ cup rum
8 ounces semi-sweet chocolate
2 tablespoons shortening

1. Lightly oil a cookie sheet.

2. Place the raisins in a bowl with the rum and add just enough hot water to cover. Let stand until the raisins are plumped, then drain and let them dry.

3. In the top of a double boiler, melt the chocolate and shortening over hot but not boiling water.

4. Remove pan from heat and add the plumped and dried raisins, tossing them thoroughly to coat.

5. With a teaspoon, drop small clusters of the candy on the prepared cookie sheet. Chill in the refrigerator, then store in an airtight container in a cool place, layered between sheets of cellophane or wax paper.

CHOCOLATE PEANUT CLUSTERS
Makes 36 clusters

8 ounces semi-sweet chocolate
1 tablespoon shortening
2 cups salted dry roast peanuts
¼ teaspoon salt

1. Lightly oil a cookie sheet.
2. In the top of a double boiler, melt the chocolate and shortening over hot but not boiling water. As soon as the chocolate is melted, remove from heat.
3. Stir in the peanuts and salt, mixing until the nuts are thoroughly coated.
4. Drop the clusters by spoonfuls onto the prepared cookie sheet and refrigerate until hard. Store in a tightly covered container in a cool place, layered between sheets of cellophane or wax paper.

CHOCOLATE POPCORN CLUSTERS
Makes ¾ pound

8 ounces semi-sweet chocolate
1 tablespoon shortening
2 cups popcorn
1 cup coarsely chopped nuts

1. Lightly oil a cookie sheet.

2. In the top of a double boiler, melt the chocolate and shortening over hot but not boiling water.

3. In a large bowl, mix the popcorn and nuts, then pour the melted chocolate mixture over and toss thoroughly.

4. Spoon the candy in clusters onto the prepared sheet and cool in the refrigerator. Store in a tightly covered container in a cool place, layered between sheets of cellophane or wax paper.

CHOCOLATE CARAMEL BUTTERFLIES
Makes 50 butterflies

Caramel, nuts, and chocolate in a new toothsome shape.

1 pound soft caramels
3 tablespoons heavy cream
1 tablespoon butter
2 cups whole unblanched almonds
12 ounces semi-sweet chocolate bits
2 tablespoons shortening

1. Lightly oil 2 cookie sheets.

2. In the top of a double boiler, melt the caramels with the cream and butter over hot water.

3. Mold a teaspoon of the caramel mixture into a ball for the body of each butterfly, and insert 4 almonds for wings. Press flat on prepared cookie sheets. Repeat until caramel is used. Let cool.

4. In the top of a double boiler, melt the chocolate and

shortening over hot water and stir until smooth. Let cool slightly, then spread over the caramel bodies of the butterflies, leaving the almond wings uncovered. Store in a tightly covered container in a cool place, layered between sheets of cellophane or wax paper.

CARAMEL NUT CHEWS
Makes sixty-four 1-inch squares

Superb soft chewy caramels.

2 cups sugar
1 cup light corn syrup
½ cup butter, softened
2 cups evaporated milk
1 cup finely chopped walnuts
1 teaspoon vanilla

1. Butter an 8-inch square pan.
2. In a heavy saucepan, combine the sugar, corn syrup, butter, and evaporated milk. Cook over medium heat, stirring constantly until mixture comes to a boil.
3. Insert candy thermometer and continue cooking and stirring until temperature reaches 245 degrees F.
4. Remove pan from heat and stir in the nuts and vanilla.
5. Pour at once into the prepared pan. Let the caramels cool slightly, then cut into 1-inch squares.
6. When completely cool, package each piece individually in plastic wrap. Store in a cool place.

TOASTED ALMOND BARK
Makes 1 pound

Simplicity of preparation makes this an ideal gift for a child to make for even the most discriminating adult taste.

1 cup unblanched almonds
8 ounces semi-sweet chocolate
2 tablespoons shortening

1. Preheat oven to 300 degrees F. and lightly butter a 9-inch square pan.
2. Toast the almonds in the oven in a shallow pan for 10 minutes. Let cool.
3. Melt the chocolate and shortening in the top of a double boiler over hot but not boiling water. As soon as the chocolate is melted, stir in the nuts and pour at once into prepared pan. Chill.
4. Break bark into irregular pieces and store in an airtight container.

MALLOWMINT BARK
Makes 1 pound

On the rocky road to candy making, we one day found ourselves with mint rather than chocolate bits, and so serendipitously created one of our children's favorite candies.

6 ounces semi-sweet chocolate bits
6 ounces chocolate mint bits
2 tablespoons shortening
1 cup mini marshmallows
½ cup nuts broken

1. Butter an 8-inch square pan.
2. Melt the chocolate with shortening in the top of a double boiler over hot but not boiling water.
3. Pour half the chocolate mixture into the prepared pan, cover with marshmallows and nuts, and pour in the remaining chocolate. Chill.
4. When cool, break into irregular pieces and store in an airtight container in a cool place.

CHOCOLATE ALMOND CRUNCH
Makes 1 pound

The extra effort required to make this candy is well rewarded by the ultimate treat.

1 cup sugar
½ cup butter
3 tablespoons water
¼ teaspoon salt
1 cup finely chopped toasted almonds
8 ounces semi-sweet chocolate
1 tablespoon shortening

1. Butter lightly an 8×12-inch pan.
2. In a heavy saucepan, combine the sugar, butter,

water, and salt and cook over medium heat, stirring constantly until the sugar is dissolved and mixture comes to a boil.

3. Insert a candy thermometer and continue cooking until temperature reaches 290 degrees F.

4. Remove from heat and stir in ⅔ cup of the nuts. Immediately pour candy onto prepared pan and let cool.

5. Melt the chocolate with the shortening in the top of a double boiler over hot but not boiling water and spread it over the cooled candy.

6. Sprinkle the chocolate layer with the remaining ⅓ cup chopped nuts, and refrigerate until chocolate hardens.

7. Break into irregular pieces and store in an airtight container in a cool place.

PARISIAN TRUFFLES
Makes 42 balls

This elegant chocolate-nut sweet requires no cooking, making it a candy for the most inexperienced cook to present with pride.

3 tablespoons butter, softened
½ cup sifted confectioners' sugar
6 ounces semi-sweet chocolate, finely grated
1 egg yolk, beaten
2 tablespoons crème de cacao
42 whole almonds
¾ cup finely chopped almonds

1. Cream the butter well, then gradually beat in the sugar. Add the grated chocolate, egg yolk, and liqueur and beat until mixture is thoroughly combined. Refrigerate for at least ½ hour.

2. Form into bite-size balls, inserting one whole almond into the center of each. Roll in the chopped nuts.

3. Place truffles on a cookie sheet or tray and chill in refrigerator overnight. Store in an airtight container in a cool place.

VIENNESE NUT BALLS
Makes 40 balls

Another elegant confection that requires no cooking.

1½ cups finely ground pecans
½ cup superfine sugar
2 tablespoons cognac
2 tablespoons light corn syrup

1. Mix the pecans and sugar together. Add the cognac and corn syrup and mix well.

2. Shape the mixture into bite-size balls and let them dry out on a cookie sheet for a few hours.

3. Store them in an airtight container in a cool place.

CREAMY MINT BALLS
Makes 60 balls

This is the simplest mint candy to prepare and is party-ready in a coating of chocolate sprinkles.

2 tablespoons butter, softened
1 pound sifted confectioners' sugar
1 egg white
1 tablespoon heavy cream
1½ teaspoons peppermint extract
¼ teaspoon salt
Chocolate sprinkles

1. Cream the butter, then gradually add half the sugar, beating until light and fluffy.
2. Beat in the egg white, cream, peppermint extract, and salt. Gradually add the remaining sugar and continue beating until smooth and stiff.
3. Refrigerate mixture at least ½ hour.
4. Shape the mixture into bite-size balls, no more than ¾ inch in diameter, and roll in chocolate sprinkles as soon as each ball is formed.
5. Place finished candy on a cookie sheet or tray and let dry overnight.
6. Store in an airtight container and keep in a cool place.

12

Holiday Giving

HOLIDAY TIMES, even more than other gift-giving occasions, bring forth an eagerness to share with neighbors
the bounty of one's kitchen and to pass along to friends
treasured family recipes. Somehow the aroma of a fruitcake seems spicier during the Christmas season, the corn
relish tangier at Thanksgiving.

While any favorite dish will bear holiday greetings
with warmth and affection, we have assembled in this
chapter a group of recipes that are particularly appropriate for certain holidays. In general, they are the breads

and buns, sauces and relishes, cakes and cookies that surround and embellish the holiday roast, that make the
holiday table a compleat feast.

Try to package your holiday gifts in containers that
might be useful during the holiday season.

Heap Christmas candies in parfait glasses or punch
cups, pile candy logs on a porcelain perfume tray.

Arrange Christmas cookies in a steam pudding mold,
in a doll's cradle for a young child, or even in a Christmas
stocking.

Pack hard sauce in a handsome stoneware crock.

Place the *tourtière* in a domed server which can display
cheeses on the Christmas Eve buffet.

Lay loaves of stollen or fruitcake on an antique bread
board; cradle the large round gugelhupf or whiskey cake
in a punch bowl.

For Easter, pack hot cross buns in a wicker basket large
enough for warm-weather picnics. Lay a loaf or two of
kulich in a shiny window box, to be planted later with
spring flowers. Pour mint vinegar into a cut-glass cruet
to adorn the holiday table.

For a harvest of Thanksgiving gifts, fill an ironstone
tureen with brandied applesauce, and a pair of covered
crystal bowls or pretty ceramic egg coddlers with cranberry and corn relish. Place the cranberry nut loaf on a
beautiful old brass trivet and the colonial corn bread in
a square cracker basket. Bear the pecan pie proudly on a
bright orange lacquer tray, prettily garnished with autumn leaves and protected with cellophane, a delectable
gift ready for the festive board.

For Passover, fill a beautiful old tea caddy with coconut
macaroons, and for Rosh Hashanah pack a golden honey
walnut loaf in a wooden bowl; rest it on a bed of walnuts
next to an attractive nutcracker.

TOURTIÈRE
Serves 6

Tourtière is a French-Canadian meat pie, the traditional entrée of the *réveillon* feast that follows midnight Mass on Christmas Eve.

½ pound ground lean pork
½ pound ground lean beef
½ pound ground veal
¼ cup finely chopped onions
¼ teaspoon savory
¼ teaspoon allspice
Dash freshly grated nutmeg
1 bay leaf
¼ cup boiling water
Pastry for 1 two-crust 9-inch pie

1. In a heavy saucepan, combine the ground pork, beef, and veal, onions, savory, allspice, nutmeg, and bay leaf with boiling water. Simmer gently for 25 minutes, adding more water if needed to prevent sticking.

2. Remove bay leaf, cool meat, and skim off excess fat.

3. Line pie plate with half the pastry and fill with the meat mixture. Cover with the remaining sheet of pastry, seal the edges of the pie, and cut small vents in the top crust to allow steam to escape.

A NOTE   Preheat oven to 425 degrees F. and bake the *tourtière* for 30 minutes, or until crust is golden. The meat pie is traditionally served with a sweet relish, black currant wine, and strong coffee. The *tourtière* may be refrigerated a day or two, or frozen.

BRANDIED YULE LOG
Makes 4 pounds; 4 small or 2 large logs

This spectacular fruit log is best made at least a few weeks in advance so the flavors can ripen.

1 pound dried apricots
1 pound dried figs, with stems removed
½ pound pitted dates
1 pound broken pecans
¼ pound chopped crystallized ginger
¼ pound candied lemon peel
2 tablespoons light corn syrup
2 tablespoons brandy
Confectioners' sugar

1. Grind or finely chop the apricots, figs, dates, pecans, ginger, and lemon peel. Add the corn syrup and brandy and mix well.
2. Shape into four small or two large logs and roll them in confectioners' sugar.
3. Wrap logs in foil to form an airtight package.

A NOTE Slice and serve on Christmas Eve with eggnog. Keeps 2 to 3 weeks in refrigerator.

DIVINITY CARAMEL LOG
Makes four 12-inch-long logs

Count on lots of time and two pairs of willing hands to make this gooey confection.

½ cup light corn syrup
2¼ cups sugar
½ cup water
2 egg whites
1 teaspoon vanilla
⅛ teaspoon salt
1 pound caramels
1 tablespoon water
½ pound chopped nuts

1. Lightly butter a cookie sheet.
2. In a heavy saucepan, combine the corn syrup, sugar, and water and cook over medium heat, stirring, until the sugar is dissolved and the mixture comes to a boil. Insert candy thermometer and cook without stirring until the temperature reaches 250 degrees F.
3. When the syrup is almost ready, beat egg whites in a large mixer bowl until stiff, adding vanilla and salt.
4. Slowly pour hot candy into the egg whites, beating constantly until mixture is very stiff and holds its shape. Do not underbeat.
5. Divide candy into four parts and place them on the prepared cookie sheet. When cool enough to handle, shape into four logs. Refrigerate for 1 hour.

6. Melt caramels with 1 tablespoon of water in the top of a double boiler.

7. Working with one log at a time, pour caramel mixture over top of one log and sprinkle with chopped nuts. Turn the log over and coat other side with caramel and nuts. Repeat for remaining logs. Keep caramel in top of double boiler over hot water to maintain proper spreading consistency.

8. Wrap logs individually in foil or plastic wrap and store in a cool place.

A NOTE   Slice and serve, enjoy within 2 weeks.

CHOCOLATE SNOWBALLS
Makes 1½ pounds

This is a marvelous gift for children to make for family, friends, or teachers since it requires only simple cooking and a final roll in coconut.

12 ounces semi-sweet chocolate
1 can (15 ounces) sweetened condensed milk
1 teaspoon vanilla
½ cup chopped walnuts
⅛ teaspoon salt
Flaked coconut

1. Melt the chocolate in the top of a double boiler over hot but not boiling water.

2. Stir in the condensed milk, vanilla, nuts, and salt. Let cool.

3. Shape the mixture into small balls and roll each in coconut as soon as it is formed. Keep in refrigerator in an airtight container.

CHRISTMAS TREE LOLLIPOPS
Makes twelve 3-inch pops

4 cups sugar
2 cups water
1½ cups light corn syrup
½ teaspoon oil of peppermint or cinnamon
Red food coloring

1. Lightly oil a cookie sheet.
2. In a heavy saucepan, combine the sugar and water. Add the corn syrup and cook over medium heat, stirring until the sugar is dissolved and the mixture comes to a boil. Wipe the sugar crystals from the sides of the pan with a brush or damp cloth.
3. When the mixture is boiling, insert a candy thermometer and cook without stirring until the temperature reaches 290 degrees F.
4. Remove from heat and stir in the oil of peppermint or cinnamon. Add the food coloring and stir just until it is evenly distributed throughout the candy.
5. On the prepared cookie sheet, pour circles of candy about 3 inches in diameter and press a lollipop stick into each one. As the pop cools, use a skewer to poke a hole in the candy near the top and to gouge initials or draw a face on the lollipop.
6. Let lollipops cool slightly, then loosen from pan

while still warm. Thread the holes with pieces of gold cord about 8 inches long.

7. When completely cool, package lollipops individually in cellophane or plastic wrap.

A NOTE   Swing these bright red pops from the branches of your Christmas tree.

FRUITY PENUCHE
Makes 81 inch-square pieces

Brown-sugar fudge dressed up for holiday giving.

2 cups brown sugar
1 cup white sugar
1 cup light cream
¼ teaspoon salt
2 tablespoons corn syrup
¼ cup butter
1 teaspoon vanilla
½ cup chopped walnuts
¼ cup raisins
¼ cup coconut

1. Butter a 9-inch square pan.
2. In a large heavy saucepan, combine the brown and white sugar, cream, salt, and corn syrup and cook over medium heat, stirring constantly until the sugar is dissolved and the mixture comes to a boil.
3. Insert candy thermometer, lower heat, and cook un-

til temperature reaches 240 degrees F., stirring occasionally.

4. Remove pan from heat and let candy cool to lukewarm, 110 degrees F.

5. Add the butter and vanilla and beat the candy with a wooden spoon until it just begins to set. Stir in the nuts, raisins, and coconut and pour into prepared pan at once and score into 1-inch squares.

6. When cool, cut and wrap squares individually in plastic wrap. Store in an airtight container in a cool place.

ORANGE HARD SAUCE
Makes 1 cup

The uses for hard sauce multiply during the holiday season, making this orange-flavored version extremely giftworthy.

6 tablespoons butter
1½ cups sifted confectioners' sugar
2 tablespoons fresh orange juice
1 tablespoon Grand Marnier
1 teaspoon grated orange rind
1 teaspoon vanilla

1. Cream butter thoroughly, then beat in the sugar slowly until well blended and fluffy.

2. Add the remaining ingredients and mix well.

3. Chill in its gift container.

A NOTE Add a surprising fillip to steamed puddings and baked apples with a dash of orange hard sauce. Keeps refrigerated up to 1 month.

CHRISTMAS CUT-OUT COOKIES
Makes 4 dozen

This is a sturdy dough to accommodate the wreaths, stars, and other holiday shapes you may want to hang on your Christmas tree. The honey gives it good keeping qualities so the cookies last through the holiday season.

3 cups sifted flour
1 teaspoon baking soda
½ teaspoon salt
6 tablespoons butter, softened
6 tablespoons sugar
1 egg
½ cup honey
1 teaspoon vanilla

1. Preheat oven to 375 degrees F. and butter cookie sheets.
2. Sift together the flour, baking soda, and salt and set aside.
3. In a large mixing bowl, cream the butter well and gradually add the sugar, beating until light and fluffy. Mix in the egg, honey, and vanilla.
4. Stir in the dry ingredients.
5. Chill thoroughly.
6. Roll dough out to ¼-inch thickness and cut out favorite holiday shapes.
7. Bake 8 to 10 minutes, or just until golden.

CHRISTMAS GINGER CRISPS
Makes about 36 cookies

These are the old-fashioned ginger cookies of Christmas past, to be decorated with colored frosting after baking.

1 cup butter, softened
1½ cups sugar
1 cup molasses
1 egg
1 teaspoon baking soda, diluted in 1 teaspoon hot water
1½ teaspoons cinnamon
½ teaspoon allspice
½ teaspoon ground cloves
½ teaspoon ginger
4½ cups flour
½ teaspoon baking powder

1. Preheat oven to 325 degrees F. and butter cookie sheets.
2. Cream butter well, then add sugar gradually and beat until light and fluffy. Add molasses, egg, and diluted soda.
3. Combine cinnamon, allspice, cloves, and ginger, and stir into creamed mixture.
4. Sift flour and baking powder together, then add to mixture and combine well.
5. Roll dough out very thin and cut into traditional Christmas shapes, such as gingerbread men, trees, stars.
6. Bake for 8 to 10 minutes.

A NOTE These ginger cookies will stay crisp in an airtight container for several weeks.

ORANGE SPRITZ COOKIES
Makes 60 cookies

1 cup butter, softened
1 cup sugar
1 tablespoon orange juice
1 egg
Grated rind 1 orange
2½ cups flour
¼ teaspoon baking soda

1. Preheat oven to 375 degrees F.
2. Cream butter. Gradually add sugar and beat until light and fluffy. Add orange juice.
3. Beat in egg and orange rind.
4. Sift together the flour and baking soda and slowly beat into the creamed mixture.
5. Put mixture in cookie press according to manufacturer's directions and form cookies in bar or wreath shapes on an ungreased cookie sheet.
6. Bake 10 to 12 minutes.

SOUTHERN WHISKEY CAKE
Makes one 10-inch tube cake or 2 loaves

This moist rich cake is a specialty of the South. Try a little moonshine on your friends at Christmas.

1 cup raisins
1 cup chopped pitted dates
1 cup Bourbon

¾ cup butter, softened
1½ cups sugar
5 eggs
4½ cups sifted cake flour
2 teaspoons baking powder
1 teaspoon baking soda
½ teaspoon salt
Grated rind 1 lemon
2 cups chopped pecans

1. In a small bowl, combine raisins, dates, and Bourbon and let stand overnight.
2. Preheat oven to 325 degrees F., butter a 10-inch tube pan, and line it with buttered wax paper.
3. Drain dates and raisins, reserving Bourbon, and set aside.
4. In a large bowl, cream the butter well. Gradually add the sugar and continue beating until light and fluffy.
5. Beat in the eggs one at a time.
6. Sift together the flour, baking powder, soda, and salt. Add them to the creamed mixture alternately with the Bourbon.
7. Stir in the lemon rind, pecans, raisins, and dates.
8. Pour the batter into prepared pan and bake 1 hour and 50 minutes, or until the cake is nicely browned.
9. Cool cake slightly, then turn out on plate. Remove paper and pour over an additional ½ cup of Bourbon. Wrap cake tightly and let stand 2 days for flavor to ripen.

A NOTE A Bourbon-soaked cake is traditional holiday fare. It keeps well tightly wrapped up to 2 weeks and, in fact, improves with age.

TRADITIONAL HOLIDAY FRUITCAKE
Makes 2 loaves and 12 cupcakes

This dark and fruity cake is traditionally served with holiday eggnog.

½ cup chopped candied citron
½ cup chopped candied orange peel
½ cup chopped candied lemon peel
1 cup cubed candied pineapple
1 cup sliced candied red cherries
1 cup slivered dried apricots
1 cup chopped pitted dates
1 cup raisins
1 cup currants
1 cup chopped pitted prunes

Grated rind 1 orange
Grated rind 1 lemon
1 cup brandy
3 cups chopped walnuts
1¼ cups butter, softened
1¼ cups sugar
6 eggs
3 cups flour
2 teaspoons baking powder
½ teaspoon baking soda
½ teaspoon salt
1 teaspoon cinnamon
1 teaspoon allspice
1 teaspoon ginger

1. In a large bowl, combine candied citron, orange peel, lemon peel, pineapple, red cherries, apricots, dates, raisins, currants, prunes, grated orange and lemon rind, and brandy. Stir well and marinate 1 or 2 days.

2. Preheat oven to 275 degrees F. and butter two 9×5-inch loaf pans and line them with buttered paper.

3. Stir nuts into candied fruit mixture.

4. In a large bowl, cream butter well. Gradually add sugar, beating until mixture is light and fluffy.

5. Beat in the eggs one at a time.

6. Sift together the flour, baking powder, soda, salt, cinnamon, allspice, and ginger. Stir the creamed mixture into the candied fruits, and add dry ingredients. Thoroughly mix.

7. Pour the batter into the prepared loaf pans and 12 cupcake liners, filling them about two thirds full. Bake loaves about 2 hours and cupcakes 60 to 80 minutes, or until they test done.

8. Cool cakes, then remove them from loaf pans. Let mellow several days at room temperature, sprinkling additional brandy on the tops daily. Wrap cakes tightly in foil or plastic bags.

A NOTE Holiday fruitcake keeps for weeks when tightly wrapped and tastes better as it ages.

GUGELHUPF or VIENNESE COFFEE RING
Makes one 10-inch ring or gugelhupf mold

In many homes holiday mornings begin with a slice of gugelhupf, a light sweet bread from Austria.

1 package dry yeast
¾ cup warm milk
2 tablespoons granulated sugar
½ cup butter, softened
½ cup sugar
3 eggs, separated

2 teaspoons vanilla
2¾ cups sifted flour
½ teaspoon salt
½ cup raisins
Grated rind 1 lemon
Confectioners' sugar

1. Dissolve yeast in 2 tablespoons of the warm milk. Stir in the granulated sugar and set aside until mixture is foamy.

2. Cream the butter well and gradually add the sugar, beating until light and fluffy. Beat in the egg yolks and vanilla.

3. Add the yeast mixture and remaining warm milk and mix well.

4. Stir in the flour, salt, raisins, and lemon rind and beat.

5. Beat the egg whites until stiff, then fold into batter.

6. Butter a 10-inch ring or fluted gugelhupf mold well, and fill with dough. Cover with towel and put in a warm place until dough rises to top of pan, about 45 minutes.

7. Preheat oven to 375 degrees F.

8. Bake for 40 minutes, or until brown.

9. Cool slightly, then turn out on cake rack and cool completely. Dust with sifted confectioners' sugar.

A NOTE   Serve within a day or two, or freeze.

CHRISTMAS STOLLEN LOAF
Makes 2 loaves

In Europe, Christmas morning brings stollen to the breakfast table. In America, this sweet fruit-filled and frosted bread is a traditional way to greet the holidays at any time of the day.

1¼ cups milk
2 packages yeast
¼ cup warm water
1 cup sugar
8 cups flour, sifted
1½ cups butter, softened
4 eggs
1 teaspoon salt

Grated rind 1 lemon
3 tablespoons brandy
8 ounces white raisins
8 ounces blanched and
    slivered almonds
⅓ cup chopped candied
    lemon peel

Glaze
1¼ cups confectioners' sugar
¼ cup lemon juice
1 teaspoon vanilla
½ cup whole blanched almonds, for decoration
½ cup candied cherries, for decoration

1. Butter two 9×5-inch loaf pans.
2. Scald milk and set aside to cool.
3. Dissolve yeast in the warm water and add 1 table-spoon of the sugar.
4. Add the cooled milk and 1 cup of the sifted flour to the yeast mixture and place in a warm place to rise until double in bulk, about 1 hour.
5. In a large bowl, cream the butter well and gradually add the remaining sugar, beating until light and fluffy. Beat in the eggs one at a time, and add the salt, lemon rind, and brandy.
6. Toss the raisins, almonds, and lemon peel in a little of the flour, then add them, all the remaining flour, and the yeast mixture to the creamed mixture.

7. Knead dough until it is smooth and elastic, then cover with a towel and let rise in a warm place until double in bulk, about 1 hour.

8. Punch dough down and turn it out on a floured board. Shape dough into two loaves and place in prepared pans. Cover and let rise until doubled in bulk, about 45 minutes.

9. Preheat oven to 350 degrees F.

10. Bake loaves for about 45 minutes, or until done.

11. To make glaze, combine confectioners' sugar, lemon juice, and vanilla and beat until smooth. Glaze stollen when it cools and decorate with almonds and candied cherries, if desired.

A NOTE   Serve within a day or two, or freeze.

BRANDIED APPLESAUCE
Makes 4 cups

What hostess wouldn't love to serve brandied applesauce with her holiday turkey or goose!

8 cups peeled and quartered apples
2 oranges, peeled, seeded, and sliced
1 cup sugar
1 teaspoon cinnamon
1 teaspoon allspice
½ cup peach brandy

1. In a large heavy saucepan, combine the apples and orange slices with enough water just to cover fruit. Simmer until fruit is pulpy.

2. Drain fruit and sieve or put it through food mill. Add sugar, cinnamon, and allspice and simmer uncovered over low heat until thickened, stirring occasionally.

3. Remove from the heat and stir in the brandy.

A NOTE Serve over warm gingerbread.

COLONIAL CORN BREAD
Makes one 8-inch square

Because Colonial travelers on foot or horseback carried corn bread with them as a staple, this used to be known as journey cake. When travelers could eat at taverns and inns en route, the name became johnnycake, and in parts of New England corn bread is still known by that name.

1 cup yellow corn meal
1 cup all-purpose flour
¼ cup sugar
4 teaspoons baking powder
¼ teaspoon salt
2 eggs
1 cup milk
¼ cup butter, melted

1. Preheat oven to 425 degrees F. and grease, then heat, an 8-inch square pan.

2. In a large bowl, sift together the corn meal, flour, sugar, baking powder, and salt.

3. Add the eggs, milk, and melted butter and beat just until smooth.

4. Pour into prepared, preheated pan and bake for 20 to 25 minutes.

A NOTE Ideal with a Thanksgiving Day turkey, or with other traditional New England fare—baked beans, ham, frankfurters. Heat corn bread in preheated 250 degree F. oven for 12 minutes and serve warm. Serve within a day or freeze.

CORN RELISH
Makes 6 cups

Thrifty New Englanders knew many ways to enjoy their crop of corn. This relish, passed along to us by a friend in Maine, is a colorful and tasty addition to an autumn holiday table.

1 cup chopped sweet red pepper
1 cup chopped green pepper
1½ cups chopped celery
1 cup chopped onions
2 cups white vinegar
1 cup sugar
1 tablespoon salt
1 teaspoon celery seed
1 tablespoon dry mustard
½ teaspoon turmeric
4 cups whole kernel corn

1. In a large saucepan, combine the chopped red and green peppers, celery, onion, vinegar, sugar, salt, and

celery seed. Bring to a boil and simmer a few minutes, stirring occasionally.

2. Add dry mustard, turmeric, and corn and simmer 5 minutes.

3. Drain most of the liquid, leaving just enough to keep the relish moist.

A NOTE Keeps 2 to 3 weeks in refrigerator.

CRANBERRY NUT BREAD
Makes 1 loaf

The Colonial settlers called them "crane berries" because the cranes feasted on them. They could just as well be called "people berries" for the same reason. Cranberries are in season during the fall, but can be kept in the freezer all year round.

¼ cup butter, softened
1 cup sugar
1 cup orange juice
2 eggs
2½ cups flour
2½ teaspoons baking powder
½ teaspoon salt
1 teaspoon baking soda
1 cup chopped walnuts
Grated rind 1 orange
2 cups chopped fresh cranberries

1. Preheat oven to 350 degrees F. and butter and flour a 9×5-inch loaf pan.

2. In a large bowl, cream the butter and gradually add the sugar. Stir in orange juice and eggs until blended.

3. Sift flour, baking powder, salt, and soda together.

4. Add the dry ingredients to creamed mixture and blend.

5. Stir the walnuts, orange rind, and cranberries into the batter.

6. Pour batter into prepared pan and bake in preheated oven about 1 hour, or until loaf is golden. Cool in pan 15 minutes, then remove to cake rack and cool completely. Wrap tightly and store in refrigerator for 24 hours.

A NOTE   Slice thin and serve with turkey and chicken dishes, or use for tea sandwiches. Freezes well.

CRANBERRY RELISH
Makes 3 cups

No holiday turkey should come to table without a cranberry sauce. Here is the one we like—a zesty, fruity relish.

4 cups cranberries, fresh or frozen
2 cups sugar
1 cup orange juice
Juice 1 lemon
1 cinnamon stick
Dash freshly grated nutmeg
½ cup raisins

Combine all ingredients and heat to boiling, stirring constantly until sugar is dissolved. Boil until cranberries pop, about 5 minutes.

A NOTE   Garnish with a sprinkling of slivered almonds. Keeps 2 to 3 weeks in refrigerator.

SOUTHERN PECAN PIE
Makes one 9-inch pie

Very few pies travel well. This rich and nut-filled pie is a happy exception and especially welcome during the holidays.

3 eggs
¾ cup sugar
¾ cup dark corn syrup
2 tablespoons melted butter
2 teaspoons vanilla
1¾ tablespoons flour
½ teaspoon salt
1 cup pecans
1 baked pie shell (9-inch)

1. Preheat oven to 350 degrees F.
2. Beat eggs until light and fluffy. Continue beating and add the sugar, corn syrup, butter, vanilla, flour, and salt. Mix well.
3. Fold in the pecans and pour mixture into prebaked pie shell.
4. Bake for 45 minutes or until firm.

HOT CROSS BUNS
Makes 12 buns

A delightful Easter bread, these buns were customarily eaten in eighteenth-century England on Good Friday only, but their popularity in America has extended the traditional season through Lent. The bun is named for the cross shape which is pressed into the raw dough before baking.

1 package yeast
2 tablespoons warm water
½ cup currants
¼ cup candied lemon peel
4 cups flour
⅓ cup butter, softened
⅓ cup sugar
1 cup milk, scalded
2 eggs
¼ teaspoon salt
½ teaspoon allspice
1 teaspoon cinnamon

Glaze
¾ cup confectioners' sugar, sifted
1 tablespoon milk
½ teaspoon vanilla

1. Butter a cookie sheet.
2. Dissolve yeast in warm water.

3. Toss the currants and candied lemon peel in ¼ cup of the flour.

4. In a large bowl, dissolve the butter and sugar in the hot scalded milk, then cool to lukewarm.

5. Add the dissolved yeast and eggs and blend well.

6. Gradually add the remaining flour and the salt, allspice, and cinnamon, then the floured lemon peel.

7. Knead the dough thoroughly, then place in a buttered bowl, cover with a towel, and let rise in a warm place for 45 minutes or until double in bulk.

8. Punch dough down and turn out onto a floured board. Divide dough into twelve balls and place on prepared cookie sheet. Cover and let rise half an hour.

9. Preheat oven to 375 degrees F.

10. With the back of a knife, press the shape of a cross into the top of each bun.

11. Bake for 25 to 30 minutes, or until buns are golden brown.

12. To make glaze, combine the confectioners' sugar, milk and vanilla and beat well. When buns are completely cool, press glaze into the cross shape on top.

A NOTE   Warm hot cross buns in preheated 250 degree F. oven for 10 minutes, taking care not to let the frosting melt. Serve within a day or two, or freeze.

KULICH (EASTER BREAD)
Makes 2 loaves

In old Russia Easter Sunday was celebrated with a feast featuring *kulich,* a feathery light and delicate loaf. The initials XV, meaning "Christ Is Risen," were shaped in the top of the loaf.

2½ cups flour
¼ cup sugar
1 teaspoon salt
Grated rind 1 lemon
1 package dry yeast
½ cup milk
¼ cup water
3 tablespoons butter, softened
1 egg
¼ cup chopped almonds
¼ cup currants

Icing
3 tablespoons warm milk
1 cup confectioners' sugar, sifted
½ teaspoon vanilla
¼ teaspoon salt
2 tablespoons slivered almonds

1. Butter two 1-pound coffee cans.
2. In a large mixing bowl, combine ¾ cup of the flour, sugar, salt, lemon rind, and dry yeast. Mix well.
3. In a saucepan, heat the milk, water, and butter until butter is melted.
4. Gradually add the melted mixture to the dry ingredients, beating at medium speed for 2 minutes.
5. Add the egg and ½ cup of the flour, beating at high speed for 2 minutes.
6. Stir in the remaining 1¼ cups flour. Turn dough out on a lightly floured board and knead until smooth

and elastic, about 10 minutes. Place dough in a greased bowl and cover. Let rise in a warm place until double in bulk, about 1 hour.

7. Punch dough down and turn out on lightly floured board. Knead in the chopped almonds and currants.

8. Divide dough in half and shape each into a ball. Press each ball into prepared coffee can. Cover and let rise in a warm place until double, about 1 hour.

9. Preheat oven to 350 degrees F.

10. Bake kulichs for 30 to 35 minutes, or until done. Remove from cans and cool on a wire rack.

11. For icing, beat the warm milk into the confectioners' sugar until smooth. Stir in the vanilla and salt.

12. When kulich is cool, frost so glaze covers top and drips down sides. Decorate with slivered almonds.

A NOTE   Serve within a day or two, or freeze.

MINT VINEGAR
Makes 2 pints

The affinity of mint for spring lamb makes this lovely vinegar appropriate as an Easter gift from the kitchen.

3¾ cups cider vinegar
1½ cups fresh mint leaves
½ cup sugar

1. In a stainless steel or enamel saucepan, bring vinegar to a boil. Add mint leaves and sugar. Stir and press mint leaves to extract flavoring, then cook for 5 minutes.

2. Pour into clean quart jar and cap tightly. Let vinegar steep for 2 weeks.

3. Place a fresh sprig of mint into two pint jars. Strain vinegar into jars and cap tightly. Store at room temperature.

A NOTE   Serve with lamb dishes, or use in a dressing for fruit salad.

COCONUT MACAROONS FOR PASSOVER
Makes 30 macaroons

3 egg whites
⅔ cup sugar
⅓ cup passover cake meal
1 can (4 ounces) flaked coconut
1 cup ground blanched almonds
Grated rind 1 lemon

1. Preheat oven to 325 degrees F. and butter cookie sheets.

2. Beat egg whites until stiff, then slowly beat in the sugar.

3. Fold in the cake meal, coconut, ground almonds, and lemon rind.

4. Drop batter by spoonfuls on prepared cookie sheets, and bake 15 minutes, or until golden.

5. Store in a cool place in an airtight container, layered between sheets of cellophane or wax paper.

HONEY WALNUT LOAF
Makes 1 loaf

Because honey signifies good fortune, this is a particularly nice gift for Rosh Hashanah, the Jewish New Year.

1 cup milk
1 cup honey
¼ cup butter, softened
½ cup packed brown sugar
2 egg yolks
2½ cups cake flour
1 teaspoon salt
1 teaspoon baking soda
¾ cup chopped walnuts
Grated rind 1 orange

1. Preheat oven to 325 degrees F. and butter and flour a 9×5-inch loaf pan.
2. Scald milk and add honey, stirring until melted. Set aside to cool.
3. In large mixing bowl, cream butter and sugar, and beat in egg yolks.
4. Sift flour with salt and soda, and add to the creamed mixture alternately with the milk mixture.
5. Stir in nuts and orange rind.
6. Pour batter into prepared pan and bake for 1 hour, or until cake is golden.

Appendix A   Mailing Food

SOME FOODS are better travelers than others. Here are some you can send safely through the mails and expect to reach their destination virtually as fresh and tasty as when they started out, barring undue delays en route.

From Chapter 2, "Nice and Easy":
  Basil Salt
  Dill Salt
  Salt aux Fines Herbes
  Seasoned Salt
  Lemon Sugar
  Orange Sugar
  Cashew Butter
  Peanut Butter
  Pralin
  Toasted Coconut
  Nutted Prunes
  Ginger Dates
  Orange Sugared Nuts
  Salted Nuts
  Spiced Walnuts

From Chapter 7, "The Relish Tray":
  All the relishes, preserves, pickles, and chutneys

From Chapter 8, "The Sauceboat":
  All-American Fudge Sauce
  Butterscotch Sauce
  Chocolate Fondue Grand Marnier
  Milk Chocolate Fondue
  Brandied Hard Sauce
  Southern Hard Sauce
  Bing Cherry Sauce
  Chinese Plum Sauce
  Cumberland Sauce
  Chili Barbecue Sauce
  Island Barbecue Sauce
  Curry Marinade
  Hawaiian Marinade
  Savory Marinade

From Chapter 9, "The Cookie Crock":
  Best Brownies
  Chocolate Almond Crisps
  Chocolate-Glazed Tea Cookies
  Cinnamon Applesauce Squares
  Date Nut Bars
  Golden Coconut Drops
  Hermits
  Koulourakia
  Molasses Snaps
  Old-Fashioned Sugar Rounds
  Peanut Butter Cookies

From Chapter 10, "The Cake Plate":
  Sweet Stanley's Chocolate Chip Cake
  Chocolate Pecan Upside Down Cake
  Spicy Jam Cake
  Gingerbread Cupcakes
  Autumn Applesauce Cake
  Spicy Banana Nut Loaf
  Lemon Loaf
  Hawaiian Nut Loaf
  Light Fruitcake

Spicy Health Loaf
Carrot Nut Ring

From Chapter 11, "The Candy Jar":
  Never-Fail Fudge
  Nut Penuche
  Pralines
  Old-Fashioned Peanut Brittle
  Mixed Nut Brittle
  Butterscotch Thins
  Crystal Mint Coins
  Lollipops
  Candied Orange Peel
  Apricot Balls

From Chapter 12, "Holiday Giving":
  Brandied Yule Log
  Divinity Caramel Log
  Christmas Tree Lollipops
  Fruity Penuche
  Orange Hard Sauce
  Orange Spritz Cookies
  Southern Whiskey Cake
  Traditional Holiday Fruitcake
  Christmas Stollen Loaf
  Cranberry Nut Bread
  Coconut Macaroons for Passover
  Honey Walnut Loaf

Packing food for mailing

For mailing, store the food in a plastic bag, then pack it well in a corrugated paper carton. Cushion the contents of the carton by surrounding with crushed styrofoam, shredded newspapers, or other material. For additional protection, you may want to pack plastic-wrapped food first in a smaller metal box before inserting into the carton. When sending several items in one carton, pack them a few inches apart and cushion well. Wrap the carton with heavy brown paper and tie it securely.

Postal regulations

You can send all kinds of food within the United States and its possessions, but check your local post office before sending food elsewhere. There are various restrictions on mailing different foods to different countries.

Send highly perishable items First Class or Air Mail (and be prepared to pay for the service). Use Parcel Post for foods that don't require rush handling, such as preserves and relishes. Ask about Parcel Post, Special Handling, which provides quicker handling than Parcel Post but not as fast as First Class Mail.

For mailing packages to servicemen stationed overseas, send packages weighing 2 pounds or less by Air Parcel Post, packages weighing up to 5 pounds by SAM (Space Available Mail), and packages weighing up to 30 pounds by PAL (Parcel Air Lift). Don't send any perishable items a long distance.

You can get insurance against loss and pilferage of food, but not for spoilage.

If you have any specific questions, consult your local postmaster.

Appendix B Sources

IF YOU CANNOT FIND CONTAINERS to suit your needs in local stores, or if you prefer to shop by mail, here are packaging sources of various kinds. Some sources have catalogues for which there is sometimes a charge.

Baskets
The Flower Cart, 3819 North Broadway, Chicago, Ill. 60613
Fran's Basket House, 89 West Main St., Rockaway, N.J. 07866
Williams-Sonoma, 576 Sutter St., San Francisco, Calif. 94102

Bottles
Bathsheba's Bottle Barn, P. O. Box 1776, Milville, N.J. 08332
Greek Island Ltd., 215 East 49 St., New York, N.Y. 10017

Home Accessories
Craft House, Colonial Williamsburg, Williamsburg, Va. 23815
Éclat, 6 Spencer Place, Scarsdale, N.Y. 10583
Old Guilford Forge, On the Green, Guilford, Conn. 06437
Seabon Scandinavian Imports, 54 East 54 St., New York, N.Y. 10022

Kitchenware
Bazaar de la Cuisine, 7–16 149 Street, Whitestone, N.Y. 11357
Bazar Français, 666 Sixth Ave., New York, N.Y. 10010
La Cuisinière, Inc., 903 Madison Ave., New York, N.Y. 10021
The Vermont Country Store, Weston, Vt. 05161

Laboratory Glass
Archer Surgical Supply, 217 East 23 St., New York, N.Y. 10010
Entropy Design, 235 East 51 St., New York, N.Y. 10022

Lucite Containers
Lucidity, 959 Second Ave., New York, N.Y. 10022

Mail Order Houses
Casual Living, Rte. 6, Stony Hill, Bethel, Conn. 06801
Edith Chapman, Rte. 303, Blauvelt, N.Y. 10913
Clarion Products, P. O. Box 189, Highland Park, Ill. 60035
Downs & Co., 1014 Davis St., Evanston, Ill. 60204
The Ferry House, 554 N. State Road, Briarcliff Manor, N.Y. 10510
Helen Gallagher-Foster House, Peoria, Ill. 61601
Sleepy Hollow Gifts, 3023 Crane Drive, Falls Church, Va. 22042
Sunset House, Sunset Bldg., Beverly Hills, Calif. 90213

Personalized Labels
Miles Kimball, Bond St., Oshkosh, Wis. 54901

Index

Accessories for containers, 4
  sources of, 285
All-American Fudge Sauce, 155
Almond(s)
  Bark, Toasted, 246
  Crescents, 183
  Crisps, Chocolate, 189
  Crunch, Chocolate, 247–48
  Pralin, 29
Anadama Raisin Bread, 85–86
Anchovy
  Butter, 19
  Spread, 44
Apple Chutney, 140
Applesauce
  Brandied, 268–69
  Cake, Autumn, 215–16
  Muffins, 92–93
  Squares, Cinnamon, 192–93
Apricot
  Balls, 241–42
  Pastry Crescents, 183–84
  Walnut Conserve, 130
Autumn Applesauce Cake, 215–16

Bacon Corn Sticks, 95
Baguettes, Continental, 84–85
Banana Nut Loaf, 216–17
Barbecue Sauces, 173
  Chili, 173
  Island, 173

Basil
  Green Beans, 144
  Salt, 14
  Vinegar, 26–27
Baskets, sources of, 285
Beans, Basil Green, 144
Bear Paws, 185
Beef
  Chili con Carne, 109–10
  Fondue Sauces, 171–73
    Horseradish, 171
    Mustard, 171–72
    Tomato Curry, 172
  Goulash, Viennese, 107–8
  Lasagna, 113–14
  Meatballs, Sweet and Sour, 59–
    60
  Meatballs in Tomato Sauce,
    112–13
  Pot Roast, Savory, 106–7
  Stew Neapolitan, 108–9
  Stuffed Cabbage, 110–11
  Tourtière with, 253
Beets, Pickled, 145
Bercy Butter, 20
Best Brownies, 186
Beurres Composés, 19–25
Bing Cherry Sauce, 165
Blueberry
  Muffins, 94
  Peach Preserve, Spicy, 132

Blue Cheese
  Ball, Danish, 47
  or Roquefort Butter, 25
Blue Plum Chutney, 141
Bottles, sources of, 285
Boxes, 6
Brandied
  Applesauce, 268–69
  Hard Sauce, 163
  Yule Log, 254
Bread, 75–96
  Anadama Raisin, 85–86
  Applesauce Muffins, 92–93
  Bacon Corn Sticks, 95
  Baguettes, Continental, 84–85
  Blueberry Muffins, 94
  Brioche, Easy, 89–91
  Challah, 81–82
  Cheese, Country, 78–79
  Cheese Twists, Parmesan, 91–92
  Coffee Ring, Viennese, 265–66
  Corn
    Colonial, 269–70
    Sticks, Bacon, 95
  Cornell, 88–89
  Cranberry Nut, 271–72
  Croutons, 11–13
  Dilly Onion, 81–82
  Easter (Kulich), 275–77
  Egg Twist, Seeded, 81–82
  Herb, Savory, 79–80
  Hot Cross Buns, 274–75
  Onion, Dilly, 81–82
  Raisin, Anadama, 85–86
  Rye, Swedish, 86–87
  Sally Lunn, 77–78
  Scones, 96
  Stollen Loaf, Christmas, 266–68
Bridge Assortment (Cookies), 187–88
Brioche, Easy, 89–91

Brownie(s)
  Best, 186
  Cupcakes, Frosted, 210–12
Butter-Nut Crisps, 188
Butters, 17–25
  Anchovy, 19
  Bercy, 20
  Cashew, 17
  Cold Flavored, 19–25
  Garlic, 21
  Honey, 21
  Lemon Herb, 22
  Maître d'Hôtel, 22–23
  Marchand de Vin, 23–24
  Mustard, 24
  Orange, 24–25
  Peanut, 17–18
  Roquefort, 25
Butterscotch
  Sauce, 156
  Thins, 237–38

Cabbage, Stuffed, 110–11
Cakes, 205–30
  Applesauce, Autumn, 215–16
  Banana Nut Loaf, 216–17
  Brownie Cupcakes, Frosted, 210–12
  Carrot Nut Ring, 229–30
  Chocolate
    Brownie Cupcakes, 210–12
    Chip, 208–9
    Fudge, 207–8
    Pecan Upside Down, 209–10
  Fruitcake
    California, 217–18
    Light, 221–22
    Traditional Holiday, 264–65
  Fudge, Favorite, 207–8
  Gingerbread Cupcakes, 214–15
  Health Loaf, Spicy, 228–29
  Honey Walnut Loaf, 278

Jam, Spicy, 212–13
Lemon Loaf, 218–19
Linzertorte, 222–23
Nut Loaf, Hawaiian, 219–20
Nut Loaf, Spicy Banana, 216–17
Nut Ring, Carrot, 229–30
Orange Rum, 223–24
Pecan Coffee Cake, 224–25
Pecan Upside Down, Chocolate, 210
Pound, Traditional, 213–14
Pound, Yogurt, 227–28
Rum, Orange, 223–24
Sour Cream Coffee Cake, 226–27
Walnut Loaf, Honey, 278
Walnut Loaf, Spicy Banana, 216–17
Walnut Ring, Carrot, 229–30
Whiskey, Southern, 262–63
Yogurt Pound, 227–28
California Fruitcake, 217–18
Camembert Log, 46
Candy, 231–50
Almond Bark, Toasted, 246
Almond Crunch, Chocolate, 247–48
Apricot Balls, 241–42
Butterscotch Thins, 237–38
Caramel Butterflies, Chocolate, 244–45
Caramel Nut Chews, 245
Chocolate
Almond Bark, Toasted, 246
Almond Crunch, 247–48
Caramel Butterflies, 244–45
Fudge, Never-Fail, 233
Mallowmint Bark, 246–47
Peanut Clusters, 243
Popcorn Clusters, 243–44
Truffles, Parisian, 248–49
Fruity Penuche, 258–59

Fudge
Fruity Penuche, 258–59
Never-Fail, 233
Nut Penuche, 234
Pralines, 235
Lollipops, 239–40
Christmas Tree, 257–58
Mallowmint Bark, 246–47
Mint Balls, Creamy, 250
Mint Coins, Crystal, 238–39
Nut Balls, Viennese, 249
Nut Brittle, Mixed, 236–37
Nut Chews, Caramel, 245
Nut Penuche, 234
Orange Peel, Candied, 240–41
Peanut Brittle, Old-Fashioned, 236
Peanut Clusters, Chocolate, 243
Penuche, Fruity, 258–59
Penuche, Nut, 234
Popcorn Clusters, Chocolate, 243–44
Pralines, 235
Rum Raisin Drops, 242
Truffles, Parisian, 248–49
See also Confections
Cans, for packaging, 5
Caramel
Butterflies, Chocolate, 244–45
Log, Divinity, 255–56
Nut Chews, 245
Carrot
Nut Ring, 229–30
Sticks, Pickled, 145–46
Cashew Butter, 17
Cauliflower Florets, Pickled, 146–47
Challah, 81–82
Cheddar Cheese
Bread, Country, 78–79
Rounds, 47–48

Cheese
  Ball, Danish, 47
  Bread, Country, 78–79
  Butter, Roquefort, 25
  Croutons, Parmesan, 11
  Liptauer Käse, 45
  Log, Camembert, 46
  Rounds, Cheddar, 47–48
  Twists, Parmesan, 91–92
Cherry Sauce, Bing, 165
Chicken
  Basque, 100–1
  Crêpes Florentine, 104–5
  Liver Pâté, 40
  à la Normande, 39
  Mulligatawny Soup, 67–68
  Orientale, 101–2
  in-the-Pot, 68–69
  Potpie, 103–4
  Salad Supreme, 124
Chili
  Barbecue Sauce, 173
  con Carne, 109–10
Chinese Plum Sauce, 166
Chocolate
  Cakes
    Brownie Cupcakes, Frosted,
      210–12
    Chip, Sweet Stanley's, 208–9
    Fudge, Favorite, 207–8
    Pecan Upside Down, 209–10
  Candy
    Almond Bark, Toasted, 246
    Almond Crunch, 247–48
    Caramel Butterflies, 244–45
    Fudge, Never-Fail, 233
    Mallowmint Bark, 246–47
    Peanut Clusters, 243
    Popcorn Clusters, 243–44
    Truffles, Parisian, 248–49
  Cookies
    Almond Crisps, 189

  -Glazed Tea, 190–91
    Meringue Puffs, 191–92
  Fondues, 157–58
    Grand Marnier, 157
    Milk, 158
  Sauce, Fudge, 155
  Snowballs, 256–57
Christmas
  Cut-Out Cookies, 260
  Ginger Crisps, 261
  Stollen Loaf, 266–68
  Tree Lollipops, 257–58
Chutneys, 140–43
  Apple, 140
  Blue Plum, 141
  Cranberry, 142
  Dried Fruit, 142–43
Cinnamon Applesauce Squares,
    192–93
Citrus Sugars, 16
  Lemon, 16
  Orange, 16
Coconut
  Drops, Golden, 195
  Macaroons, 278
  Oatmeal Crisps, 193–94
  Toasted, 29–30
Coffee
  Cake
    Pecan, 224–25
    Sour Cream, 226–27
  Ring, Viennese, 265–66
Colonial Corn Bread, 269–70
Confections, 31–34
  Brandied Yule Log, 254
  Chocolate Snowballs, 256–57
  Divinity Caramel Log, 255–56
  Ginger Dates, 31–32
  Nutted Prunes, 31
  Orange Sugared Nuts, 32
  Pralin, 29
  Salted Nuts, 33

Spiced Walnuts, 33–34
Toasted Coconut, 29–30
See also Candy
Conserves
Apricot Walnut, 130
Plum Nut, 131
Containers, 1–6. *See also* specific foods
accessories, 4
cookware and kitchen accessories, 2–3
from the florist, 4
miscellaneous, 4
packaging, 5–6
serving pieces, 3
sources, 285–86
toys, 4
Continental Baguettes, 84–85
Cookies, 181–203
Almond Crescents, 183
Almond Crisps, Chocolate, 189
Applesauce Squares, Cinnamon, 192–93
Apricot Pastry Crescents, 183–84
Bear Paws, 185
Bridge Assortment, 187–88
Brownies, Best, 186
Butter-Nut Crisps, 188
Chocolate
Almond Crisps, 189
Brownies, 186
-Glazed Tea, 190–91
Meringue Puffs, 191–92
Cinnamon Applesauce Squares, 192–93
Coconut Drops, Golden, 195
Coconut Macaroons, 278
Coconut Oatmeal Crisps, 193–94
Cut-Out, Christmas, 260
Date Nut Bars, 194–95
Ginger Crisps, Christmas, 261
Hermits, 196–97

Koulourakia, 197–98
Madeleines, 198–99
Meringue Puffs, Chocolate, 191–92
Molasses Snaps, 199–200
Oatmeal Crisps, Coconut, 193–94
Orange Spritz, 202
Peanut Butter, 201–2
Pecan Snowballs, 202–3
Sugar Rounds, Old-Fashioned, 200–1
Walnut Bars, Date, 194–95
Walnut Crisps, Butter, 188
Cookware, for containers, 2–3
Corn
Bread, Colonial, 269–70
Relish, 270–71
Sticks, Bacon, 95
Cornell Bread, 88–89
Country
Cheese Bread, 78–79
Pâté, 41–42
Crab Meat Remoulade, 49
Cranberry
Chutney, 142
Nut Bread, 271–72
Relish, 272–73
Creamy Mint Balls, 250
Crêpes Florentine, Chicken, 104–5
Croutons, 11–13
Garlic, 12
Herbed, 12–13
Parmesan, 11
Crystal Mint Coins, 238–39
Cumberland Sauce, 166–67
Cupcakes
Frosted Brownie, 210–12
Gingerbread, 214–15
Curried Shrimp Spread, 42–43
Curry
Marinade, 178

Mayonnaise, 175
Sauce, Tomato, 172

Danish Cheese Ball, 47
Date(s)
  Ginger, 31–32
  Nut Bars, 194–95
Dill
  Mayonnaise, 176
  Pesto Sauce, 49–50
  Salt, 14
Dilly Onion Bread, 81–82
Divinity Caramel Log, 255–56
Duxelles, 10

Easter Bread (Kulich), 275–76
Eggplant, Moussaka of, 115–16
Egg Twist, Seeded, 81–82
English Lemon Curd, 158–59

Favorite Fudge Cake, 207–8
Florists' accessories for contain-
  ers, 4
Fondue
  Beef, Sauces, 171–72
    Horseradish, 171
    Mustard, 171–72
    Tomato Curry, 172
  Chocolate, Grand Marnier, 157
  Chocolate, Milk, 158
Fruitcake
  California, 217–18
  Light, 221–22
  Traditional Holiday, 264–65
Fruit
  Chutney, Dried, 142–43
  Log, Brandied Yule, 254
  Marmalade, Mixed, 134–35
  Sauces, 160–62
Fruity Penuche, 258–59
Fudge
  Cake, Favorite, 207–8

Fruity Penuche, 258–59
Never-Fail, 233
Nut Penuche, 234
Pralines, 235
Sauce, All-American, 155

Garlic
  Butter, 21
  Croutons, 12
  Vinegar, 28
Gazpacho, 71–72
Gingerbread Cupcakes, 214–15
Ginger
  Crisps, Christmas, 261
  Dates, 31–32
Glazes
  Chocolate, 190–91
  for Stollen Loaf, 267, 268
Golden Coconut Drops, 195
Goulash, Viennese, 107–8
Green Beans, Basil, 144
Green Tomato Relish, 148
Gugelhupf, 265–66

Ham, Spinach Salad with Mush-
  rooms and, 126
Hard Sauces, 163–64
  Brandied, 163
  Orange, 259
  Southern, 163–64
Hawaiian Marinade, 178–79
Hawaiian Nut Loaf, 219–20
Health Loaf, Spicy, 228–29
Herb
  Bread, Savory, 79–80
  Butter, Lemon, 22
Herbed Croutons, 13
Herbed Salts, 14–15
  Basil, 14
  Dill, 14
  aux Fines Herbes, 15

Herbed Vinegars, 26–28
  Basil, 26–27
  Garlic, 28
  Mixed, 27
  Tarragon, 26
Hermits, 196–97
Hollandaise, Mock, 174
Home accessories for containers, 4
  sources of, 285
Honey
  Butter, 21
  Orange Slices, 133–34
  Walnut Loaf, 279
Hors d'Oeuvres, 37–60
  Anchovy Spread, 44
  Camembert Log, 46
  Cheddar Cheese Rounds, 47–48
  Cheese Blends, 45–48
  Chicken Liver Pâtés, 39–40
  Cold Mixed Vegetables, 52–55
  Country Pâté, 41–42
  Crab Meat Remoulade, 49
  Curried Shrimp Spread, 42–43
  Danish Cheese Ball, 47
  Liptauer Käse, 45
  Meatballs, Sweet and Sour, 59–60
  Mushrooms, Marinated, 51–52
  Olives, Marinated Cocktail, 50
  Pâtés, 39–42
  Pizza Quiche, 57–58
  Ratatouille, 54–55
  Salade Méditerranée, 53–54
  Salmon Quiche, 56
  Salmon Spread, Smoked, 43–44
  Shrimp in Pesto Sauce, 49–50
  Shrimp Spread, Curried, 42–43
  Sweet and Sour Meatballs, 59–60
  Vegetables Vinaigrette, 52–53
Horseradish Sauce, 171
Hot Cross Buns, 274–75

Icing. *See also* Cakes
  Kulich, 275–77
Island Barbecue Sauce, 173

Jam Cake, Spicy, 212–13

Kitchen accessories for containers, 2–3
  sources of, 285
Koulourakia, 197–98
Kulich, 275–77

Labels, 5
  source for, 286
Laboratory glass, sources for, 286
Lamb
  Moussaka, 115–16
  Romanoff, 117–18
Lasagna, 113–14
Lemon
  Curd, English, 158–59
  Herb Butter, 22
  Loaf, 218–19
  Sugar, 16
Lime Preserve, Tomato, 133
Linzertorte, 222–23
Liptauer Käse, 45
Liver Pâté, Chicken, 40
  á la Normande, 39
Lollipops, 239–40
  Christmas Tree, 257–58
Lucite containers, source for, 286

Macadamia Nut Loaf, Hawaiian, 219–20
Macaroons, Coconut, 278
Madeira Sauce, Piquant, 167–68
Madeleines, 198–99
Mailing of food, 281–84
Mail order houses, 286
Maître d'Hôtel Butter, 22–23
Mallowmint Bark, 246–47

Marchand de Vin Butter, 23–24
Marinades, 178–79
  Curry, 178
  Hawaiian, 178–79
  Savory, 179
Marmalade, Mixed Fruit, 134–35
Mayonnaises, Flavored, 175–77
  Curry, 175
  Dill, 176
  Remoulade Sauce, 176–77
Meat. *See also* Beef
  Sauces for, 165–70
  Tourtière (Pie), 253
Meatballs
  Sweet and Sour, 59–60
  in Tomato Sauce, 112–13
Melon Rind, Spiced, 136–37
Meringue Puffs, Chocolate, 191–92
Milk Chocolate Fondue, 158
Minestrone, Piedmont, 69–70
Mint
  Balls, Creamy, 250
  Coins, Crystal, 238–39
  Vinegar, 277–78
Molasses Snaps, 199–200
Moussaka, 115–16
Muffins
  Applesauce, 92–93
  Blueberry, 94
Mulligatawny Soup, 67–68
Mushroom(s)
  Duxelles, 10
  Marinated, 51–52
  Soup, 63–64
  Spinach Salad with Ham and,
    126
Mustard
  Butter, 24
  Sauce, 171–72

Never-Fail Fudge, 233
Newsprint, for wrapping, 6

Nut(s). *See also* specific kinds
  Balls, Viennese, 249
  Bread, Cranberry, 271–72
  Brittle, Mixed, 236–37
  Butters, 17–18
    Cashew, 17
    Peanut, 17–18
  Chews, Caramel, 245
  Loaf, Hawaiian, 219–20
  Orange Sugared, 32
  Penuche, 234
  Salted, 33
Nutted Prunes, 31

Oatmeal Crisps, Coconut, 193–94
Old Fashioned
  Peanut Brittle, 236
  Sugar Rounds, 200–1
Olives, Marinated Cocktail, 50
Onion
  Bread, Dilly, 81–82
  Soup, 65
Orange
  Butter, 24–25
  Hard Sauce, 259
  Peel, Candied, 240–41
  Rum Cake, 223–24
  Slices, Honey, 133–34
  Soup, 72
  Spritz Cookies, 262
  Sugar, 16
  Sugared Nuts, 32

Packaging, 5–6. *See also* specific
  foods
  sources for, 285–86
Parisian Truffles, 248–49
Parmesan Cheese Twists, 91–92
Parmesan Croutons, 11
Pâtés, 39–42
  Chicken Liver, 40
    à la Normande, 39
  Country, 41–42

Peach(es)
Jam, Plum, 130–31
Preserve, Spicy Blueberry, 132
Sauce, Fresh, 160
Spiced, 137–38
Peanut
Brittle, Old-Fashioned, 236
Butter, 17–18
Cookies, 201–2
Clusters, Chocolate, 243
Pears in Madeira, 135–36
Pea Soup, Split, 66
Pecan(s)
Balls, Viennese Nut, 249
Cake, Chocolate Upside Down,
210
Coffee Cake, 224–25
Orange Sugared, 32
Pie, Southern, 273
Snowballs, 202–3
Penuche
Fruity, 258–59
Nut, 234
Pepper Relish, Sweet Mixed, 150
Pesto (Sauce)
Dill, 49–50
Genovese, 9
Piccalilli, Piccadilly, 149
Pickled Vegetables, 144–47
Beets, 145
Carrot Sticks, 145–46
Cauliflower Florets, 146–47
Green Beans, Basil, 144
Piedmont Minestrone, 69–70
Pies. *See also* Quiches
Chicken Potpie, 103–4
Meat, Tourtière, 253
Pecan, Southern, 273
Pineapple
in Kirsch, Fresh, 161
Sticks, Spiced, 138–39
Piquant Madeira Sauce, 167–68

Pizza Quiche, 57–58
Plastic bags, 6
Plum
Chutney, Blue, 141
Conserve, Nut, 131
Jam, Peach, 130–31
Sauce, Chinese, 166
Soup, 73
Popcorn Clusters, Chocolate, 243–
44
Porc Bordelaise, 118–19
Pork
Bordelaise, 118–19
Pâté, Country, 41–42
Tourtière with, 253
Potato Soup, Vichyssoise, 70–71
Pot Roast, Savory, 106–7
Pouf packaging, 6
Pound Cake
Traditional, 213–14
Yogurt, 227–28
Pralin (Praline Powder), 29
Pralines, 235
Preserves
Spicy Blueberry Peach, 132
Tomato Lime, 133
Prunes, Nutted, 31

Quiches, 56–58
Pizza, 57–58
Salmon, 56

Raisin
Bread, Anadama, 85–86
Drops, Rum, 242
Ratatouille, 54–55
Relishes, 127–51
Apple Chutney, 140
Apricot Walnut Conserve, 130
Basil Green Beans, 144
Beets, Pickled, 145

Blueberry Peach Preserves, 132
Carrot Sticks, Pickled, 145–46
Cauliflower Florets, Pickled, 146–47
Chutneys, 140–43
Corn, 270–71
Cranberry, 272–73
  Chutney, 142
Fruit Chutney, Dried, 142–43
Fruit Marmalade, Mixed, 134–35
Green Beans, Basil, 144
Green Tomato, 148
Honey Orange Slices, 133–34
Lime Preserve, Tomato, 133
Melon Rind, Spiced, 136–37
Orange Slices, Honey, 133–34
Peaches, Spiced, 137–38
Peach Plum Jam, 130–31
Peach Preserves, Spicy Blueberry, 132
Pears in Madeira, 135–36
Pepper, Sweet Mixed, 150
Piccalilli, Piccadilly, 149
Pickled Vegetables, 144–47
Pineapple Sticks, Spiced, 138–39
Plum Chutney, Blue, 141
Plum Jam, Peach, 130–31
Plum Nut Conserve, 131
Spiced Melon Rind, 136–37
Spiced Peaches, 137–38
Spiced Pineapple Sticks, 138–39
Spicy Blueberry Peach Preserves, 132
Tomato, Green, 148
Tomato Lime Preserve, 133
Vegetable, 148–51
Zucchini, 150–51
Remoulade Sauce, 176–77
Roquefort Butter, 25
Rum

Cake, Orange, 223–24
Raisin Drops, 242
Rye Bread, Swedish, 86–87

Salade Méditerranée, 53–54
Salads
  Chicken, Supreme, 124
  Salade Méditerranée, 53–54
  Spinach, with Ham and Mushrooms, 126
  Tuna, Niçoise, 125
Sally Lunn Bread, 77–78
Salmon
  Quiche, 56
  Spread, Smoked, 43–44
Salted Nuts, 33
Salts, 14–15
  Basil, 14
  Dill, 14
  aux Fines Herbes, 15
  Seasoned, 15
Sangria, 35
Sauces, 153–79
  Barbecue, 173
  Beef Fondue, 171–73
  Bordelaise, 168–69
  Butterscotch, 156
  Cherry, Bing, 165
  Chocolate Fondue, 157–58
  Chocolate Fudge, 155
  Cumberland, 166–67
  Curry Marinade, 178
  Curry Mayonnaise, 175
  Dill Mayonnaise, 176
  Fruit, 160–62
  Fudge, All-American, 155
  Hard, 163–64
    Orange, 259
  Hollandaise, Mock, 174
  Horseradish, 171
  Lemon Curd, English, 158–59
  Madeira, Piquant, 167–68

Marinades, 178–79
Mayonnaises, Flavored, 175–77
for Meat, 165–70
Mustard, 171–72
Orange Hard, 259
Peach, Fresh, 160
Pesto, Dill, 49–50
Pesto Genovese, 9
Pineapple in Kirsch, Fresh, 161
Plum, Chinese, 166
Polonaise, 13
Remoulade, 176–77
Strawberry, 161–62
Sundae, 155–56
Tomato, 169–70
  Curry, 172
  Meatballs in, 112–13
Vinaigrette, 170
Savory
  Herb Bread, 79–80
  Marinade, 179
  Pot Roast, 106–7
Scones, 96
Sealing containers, 6
Seasoned Salt, 15
Seeded Egg Twist, 82–83
Serving pieces, for containers, 3
Shrimp
  Aegean, 123–24
  in Pesto Sauce, 49–50
  Spread, Curried, 42–43
Soups, 61–73
  Chicken, Mulligatawny, 67–68
  Chicken-in-the-Pot, 68–69
  Gazpacho, 71–72
  Minestrone, Piedmont, 69–70
  Mulligatawny, 67–68
  Mushroom, 63–64
  Onion, 65
  Orange, 72
  Pea, Split, 66
  Plum, 73

Potato, Vichyssoise, 70–71
Spinach, 64–65
Vichyssoise, 70–71
Sources, 285–86
Sour Cream Coffee Cake, 226–27
Southern Hard Sauce, 163–64
Southern Pecan Pie, 273
Southern Whiskey Cake, 262–63
Spaghetti Sauce
  Pesto Genovese, 9
  Tomato, Meatballs in, 112–13
Spiced
  Melon Rind, 136–37
  Peaches, 137–38
  Pineapple Sticks, 138–39
  Walnuts, 33–34
Spicy
  Banana Nut Loaf, 216–17
  Blueberry Peach Preserves, 132
  Health Loaf, 228–29
  Jam Cake, 212–13
Spinach
  Salad with Ham and Mushrooms, 126
  Soup, 64–65
Split Pea Soup, 66
Spreads. *See* Hors d'Oeuvres
Stollen Loaf, Christmas, 266–68
Strawberry Sauce, 161–62
Sugar Rounds, Old-Fashioned, 200–1
Sugars, Citrus, 16
  Lemon, 16
  Orange, 16
Sundae Sauces, 155–56
  Butterscotch, 156
  Fudge, 155
Swedish Rye, 86–87
Sweet and Sour Meatballs, 59–60
Sweet Stanley's Chocolate Chip Cake, 208–9

Tarragon Vinegar, 26
Tomato
  Lime Preserve, 133
  Relish, Green, 148
  Sauce, 169–70
    Curry, 172
    Meatballs in, 112–13
Tourtière, 253
Toys, for containers, 4
Truffles, Parisian, 248–49
Tuna
  Salad Niçoise, 125
  Vitello Tonnato, 121–22
Turkey Tetrazzini, 99–100

Veal
  Marengo, 120–21
  Pâté, Country, 41–42
  Vitello Tonnato, 121–22
Vegetables. *See also* Salads; Soups;
    specific vegetables
  Cold Mixed, 52–55
  Ratatouille, 54–55
  Relishes, 148–51
  Vinaigrette, 52–53
Vichyssoise, 70–71
Viennese
  Coffee Ring, 265–66
  Goulash, 107–8
  Nut Balls, 249
Vinaigrette Sauce, 170

Vinegars, Herbed, 26–28
  Basil, 26–27
  Garlic, 28
  Mint, 277–78
  Mixed, 27
  Tarragon, 26
Vitello Tonnato, 121–22

Walnut(s)
  Bars, Date Nut, 194–95
  Bread, Cranberry, 271–72
  Chews, Caramel, 245
  Conserve, Apricot, 130
  Conserve, Plum, 131
  Crisps, Butter-Nut, 188
  Loaf, Honey, 278
  Loaf, Spicy Banana, 216–17
  Orange Sugared, 32
  Penuche, 234
  Prunes with, 31
  Ring, Carrot, 229–30
  Spiced, 33–34
Whiskey Cake, Southern, 262–63
Wine
  Butter, Marchand de Vin, 23–24
  Sangria, 35

Yogurt Pound Cake, 227–28

Zucchini Relish, 150–51